NOBODY

The Untold Story of
ADRIAN ALSTON

NODDY

The Untold Story of
ADRIAN ALSTON

PHILIP MICALLEF

FAIRPLAY
PUBLISHING

First published in 2023 by Fair Play Publishing

PO Box 4101, Balgowlah Heights, NSW 2093, Australia

www.fairplaypublishing.com.au

ISBN: 978-1-925914-84-9

ISBN: 978-1-925914-85-6 (ePub)

Cover design and typesetting by Leslie Priestley

Front cover photograph of Adrian Alston from the Fair Play Collection.

All photographs are from the personal collection of Adrian Alston or the Fair Play Collection.

All inquiries should be made to the Publisher via sales@fairplaypublishing.com.au

NATIONAL
LIBRARY
OF AUSTRALIA

A catalogue record of this book is available from the National Library of Australia.

Contents

Foreword   vii

Introduction   ix

Chapter 1   It all started on the streets of Preston   1

Chapter 2   The offer that changed Alston's life   6

Chapter 3   Prawn cocktails, sun and surf   11

Chapter 4   Striker leaves his mark   16

Chapter 5   Dream call-up for Australia   21

Chapter 6   Rapid rise woos Arok, Rasic   27

Chapter 7   All eyes on the 1974 World Cup   33

Chapter 8   Socceroos savour trip of a lifetime   39

Chapter 9   Alston the centre of attention   44

Chapter 10   In the court of football royalty   49

Chapter 11   Rasic unleashes his 'three gangsters'   54

Chapter 12   Alston snubs Bundesliga   59

Chapter 13   Career at a crossroads   64

Chapter 14   Flying the flag for Australia   69

Chapter 15   Noddy answers SOS call   74

Chapter 16   An American dream is crushed   79

Chapter 17   Warren and Wilson, the born leaders   84

Chapter 18   Lifting the gloom   89

Chapter 19   Turning back the clock   94

Chapter 20   Career at a crossroads   99

Chapter 21   Alston scores his greatest goal   102

Chapter 22   The 'dream team'   106

Chapter 23   The long road from Germany to Qatar   113

Chapter 24   The last word: Thanks for everything, Boss   119

Acknowledgements   121

About the Author   122

Foreword

Adrian Alston is an incredible human being with a heart of gold.

He also happened to be a top footballer with a nose for goals and I feel privileged to have worked with him at the highest level of the game we both love.

'Noddy' of course was one of Australian football's most talented forwards who lifted the Socceroos team to some amazing heights when he was at his peak in the 1970s.

Nobody will take the 1974 World Cup qualification away from us and we owe England-born Noddy a lot for an experience in West Germany that we will never forget.

His extraordinary ability made him a marked man … not just by defenders who sought to stop him, but also by clubs that sought to sign him.

Yet he was able to concentrate on his job despite increasing media interest in the weeks leading up to the World Cup mainly because he is such a low-key person.

Remarkably, he was unfazed by it all. Or he did not let the scrutiny affect his game.

West German and British journalists, cameramen, scouts and agents were following us in the trial matches in Europe just before the tournament kicked off and he was the centre of attention.

After the World Cup, he had some serious offers and he was silly to knock back overtures from big Bundesliga clubs to sign for modest Luton Town.

He was lured to the country of his birth where he could follow in his brother Alec's footsteps, who had played for Preston North End.

It was a mistake and I think Noddy knows it.

Noddy was a popular figure within the football community and loved by the entire Socceroos squad. Firstly because he was a hell of a footballer and secondly due to his happy-go-lucky character. In a way, he was the life of the squad.

He is a super-confident person and that quality came across in the way he played his football.

People sometimes mistook his cockiness for arrogance, but I tell you, Noddy would not even know what arrogance means.

After he retired from football, he worked for many years with people with a disability and that tells you everything you need to know about this most generous and very special man.

Rale Rasic, OAM
Australia's 1974 World Cup coach

Introduction

The stories surrounding a bunch of gallant Socceroos who dared to dream and were rewarded with a journey of a lifetime in 1973 and 1974 are plentiful and colourful.

None more so than that of Adrian Alston, the flamboyant forward who came to Australia in the late 1960s as an unknown and became one of the country's finest and most popular strikers.

When it was suggested to me that I should write a biography of the man affectionately known as 'Noddy', I knew all along that the World Cup star who has the gift of the gab would jump on the opportunity to tell his story in book form.

As a high-profile player, Noddy was always a much loved figure as far as the media was concerned.

I have known Noddy for decades and have always regarded him as a bloke who is opinionated, cocky, entertaining and, above all, fair dinkum.

What you see is what you get with Noddy.

But throughout his football journey that took him from the streets of dreary Preston in the north of England to the bright lights of the World Cup in West Germany, he always retained a sense of respect for, and gratitude to, the many people who helped him realise his lofty aspirations.

Throughout the many conversations we had to prepare this book, Noddy always insisted on acknowledging all those who helped him along the way.

From committee members, coaches, teammates, supporters and last but not least, his wife, Doreen, who played the difficult role of 'footballer's wife' with dedication, loyalty and perseverance.

Alston's is a feel-good story that warms the heart and makes you realise that nothing is impossible in life if you are prepared to listen to the little voice in your head, back yourself and have a go.

He knew all along that there would be speed humps to overcome and unexpected detours to negotiate, but he only looked at the destination.

He got there in the end and Australian football will be forever grateful.

Chapter 1
It all started on the streets of Preston

Football was enjoying massive popularity in the Lancashire city of Preston in the 1950s.

England star Tom Finney was at the peak of his career and thrilled the Preston North End faithful with his fabled forward feats.

With Finney leading the way, the Lilywhites became one of the English First Division's strongest teams, finishing runners-up to Arsenal in 1953 and Wolverhampton Wanderers in 1958.

They were also FA Cup finalists against West Bromwich Albion in 1954.

Times were tough in the north of England in the decade or so after World War II and both Preston and Finney's exploits on many a Saturday afternoon gave the region a sense of pride and a reason for its people to forget their daily struggles for a while.

It was one of the finest periods in the famous club's history. Any child in the northern city who loved the 'game of the people' dreamed of one day wearing Preston's white strip at their home ground, Deepdale.

Or, better still, playing in a Cup final at Wembley.

Most players preferred to win the Cup than the League.

The FA Cup final was regarded as the highlight of the English football season before the European Cup juggernaut came along in the latter half of the 1950s and changed everything.

One such besotted child was a certain Adrian Alston, who was the third son of a professional boxer. He was born on 6 February 1948 to Alec and Ann and would fall in love with the game not too long after he learned how to walk.

Alston's older siblings, Alec and Alan, were sporty types too but they channelled their interest in different ways.

"Believe it or not, my father was the seventh son of the seventh son, which was amazing, even in those days," said Alston, who lives in Unanderra, south of Wollongong on the New South Wales (NSW) south coast.

"My eldest brother Alec played for Preston with the great Finney. He died at 71 years of age through head trauma from football. My other brother Alan was a motor mechanic and used to race in Formula Four. Alan looked after me very well when I was young and to this day, he's my best friend. He lives in Australia in a township called Wongawilli which is a 15-minute drive from Unanderra."

Coming from such a sporting family, football-lover Adrian was never going to be the odd man out and let the 'A' team down (all his immediate family's initials were AA). He would play and watch the game as often as possible. Before long, his love for football became an unbridled passion.

"Life was not easy yet in a way it was good because we did not know any better. Looking back, however, I sometimes wonder how we managed as a family," he recalled.

"As far as I was concerned, I had a happy childhood … playing the game I loved. I played my first football in the streets at six or seven years of age.

"We had no gardens them days, just streets. One day Alan kicked the ball so hard and so badly that he broke a window of a nearby house. The owner would not give me my ball back, so that was the last time I played with my brother."

The future Socceroos' star started playing organised football from 11 years onwards with Trinity Secondary School in Preston.

He then played in the district leagues with his friends from the Ribbleton area where he grew up.

Before long, he was noticed by Preston North End youth and suddenly, he was not Adrian Alston anymore but 'Alec Alston's brother'. He signed up and played for the youth B team.

"I was 16 or 17 and signed as an amateur—I was never a pro with Preston—and I think in one of the reserves games I scored against Everton, but unfortunately we lost 7–1. Centre-forward Joe Royle, who would become a Goodison Park legend and England international, scored about five or six, I think," he said.

"It was quite funny really because there was a guy called Willie Cunningham who was a Scottish international in the mid-50s and who played in the team with my brother and Finney. He was one of the coaches at Preston and we used to train at night—not during the day because we were only amateurs—and I was there for nearly a season before he came up to me one day with some bad news that I was not expecting. He told me I had to leave the club because I was not big enough and strong enough and stuff like that." (More on this in Chapter 2.)

"I did not believe him. He told me I did not play like my brother Alec and I responded, 'Exactly, we are completely different players. He is a strong and direct forward whereas I like to dribble and take on defenders'.

"I was never the sort of guy to let anybody tell me I would not make it, anyway. I was determined to become a professional footballer and nobody was going to change me."

Adrian's brother Alec was 11 years older than him and already playing first grade for

Preston by the time the youngest Alston was 18. He used to go to the games and watch Alec play. The eldest Alston was a forward and that is probably why Adrian became a striker. Alec was his idol, after all. Apart from local hero Finney, of course.

Alston was short and skinny in his younger days … basically he was not exactly the perfect example of a typical English forward in the 1960s.

But he soon got the break that would transform his career and subsequently change the fortunes of the game on the other side of the world.

The great Jim Kelly, who had played for Blackpool alongside Stanley Matthews on a tour of Australia in 1958 and who lived in Blackpool, was coaching non-league team Fleetwood and after watching Alston play for Preston, he told his brother Alec—who was then a Fleetwood player—that he wanted to sign the young man and take him all the way to Australia.

"When my brother told me about this I said, 'What would I want to go to Australia for?' He said this fellow (Kelly) wanted me to sign. I said, 'I will sign … but for Fleetwood', because Preston did not want me."

Alston duly joined Fleetwood in 1967 and played a handful of games, one of them being a Lancashire Cup tie against Kelly's former club Blackpool. He scored in a 1–0 win.

At that point Kelly let Alston know that he was going to Australia in two months. He insisted that he wanted Alston to be on the plane with him. Alston was still unconvinced and reiterated his dim view of such a big and bold step. All he wanted to do was play football in England, not go on a journey into the unknown on the other side of the world.

But Kelly knew what he was talking about and what he was doing, firstly because he had seen Alston's skill in person, and secondly, he had played in Australia for South Coast United from 1961 to 1965. During that time he also coached the Illawarra club south of Sydney and had a brief stint as Australia's national team coach. He was convinced that Alston's game would flourish 'down under'.

He explained to Alston that the grounds in Australia would suit him. "They are hard, bumpy and solid like rock but … guess what? They are dry," he told him.

Alston was quick even at that early stage of his career. He loved nothing more than running at defenders with the ball at his feet and he was sold on the idea of going to Australia when Kelly promised him, "Believe me, son, you'll do well there". The rest is history.

So one minute Alston was on five pounds a week with non-league team Fleetwood and the next he was offered $60 (30 pounds) a week to play in Australia. At that point, he thought, *Here we go*. He discussed the tempting offer with his girlfriend, Doreen Emmerson—who is now his wife—and his family but up to the very end his father kept telling him, "You won't go, you won't leave us". That's how much he did not want his son to leave. He did not want to lose him.

Alec senior was the type of supportive parent who would watch his sons play whenever or wherever he could. He hardly ever missed a big game. It goes without saying that he later went to West Germany to watch Adrian play in the 1974 World Cup.

"One day in season 1974–75 when I was with Luton Town, we were playing Birmingham City away and my brother Alan brought Dad to the game to watch me play," he said.

"After the game, we noticed an ambulance outside the ground. I told my teammates, 'I bet that's my dad, he's hit somebody'. Gospel truth, my dad broke somebody's jaw because this guy had the temerity to say in front of him that I was shit. This after I had scored two goals in a 4–1 win over a team that had future England striker Trevor Francis in their line-up. By then my dad would have been bragging off, saying 'that's my son', and he must have taken offence to the fan's comment, so he hit him. That's my dad for you."

In the early 1980s, Alston's parents migrated to Australia which is where they both died.

Alston came to Australia at the height of summer—28 January 1968—and signed for South Coast United who played in the NSW Division One. Kelly was going to coach the team. They played their home games in Woonona, north of Wollongong. The ground is no more as the area has become a very expensive housing estate.

So how did he and his girlfriend Doreen sort out the little matter of him moving to the other side of the world?

The two lovebirds were forced into a temporary split. Doreen did not travel to Australia with her boyfriend because he was coming for only one season—a six-month loan—that would end in September, or thereabouts anyway. He was going to be home for Christmas, after all. Or so they thought.

Happy-go-lucky Alston very much liked what he saw in Australia, particularly the laid-back lifestyle, and he just knew within two weeks that South Coast were pleased with his performances and wanted him to stay on beyond the loan period … and he wanted to stay too.

He was not going back home anytime soon.

"After four weeks of being here, I wrote to Doreen—there were no mobile phones in the 1960s—and begged her to come over and have a look at the country. She was in love with me and vice versa, so I wanted us to be together. We talked about it and we decided to give it a go. So she went down to the embassy and applied for a permit to emigrate to Australia. Emigration of course was free [in] those days so it cost her no money to come over. We always knew we would return home if things did not work out," he remembered.

"Doreen's parents backed her to the hilt. They were wonderful people, excellent.

My parents were supportive too."

In no time, he was reunited with the love of his life and surprise, surprise, his game got better and better.

Adrian and Doreen's lives would never be the same.

Chapter 2
The offer that changed Alston's life

Ambitious Alston had every right to be confused and frustrated by the mixed messages he was receiving from some of his coaches as he made his first tentative steps in league football.

Here was a highly promising teenager with stars in his eyes who was eager to make headway in the dog-eat-dog world of the English game.

Alston was a natural attacker who loved nothing more than running with the ball and taking on burly defenders with his pace and dribbling skills.

Already at such an early age he was in the 'good to watch' category and seen by many as an entertainer in the making, but some coaches did not see it that way.

Alston's first proper club was Preston North End. He signed as an amateur in 1967 and trained at night with apprentice full-time professionals in the youth team.

Not being a professional meant he luckily avoided chores such as cleaning the pro players' boots and the dressing rooms. The club's amateurs didn't do that sort of stuff.

"I saw it as a big achievement in itself to be a Preston North End player," Alston said.

"In them days there was the senior first team and the second team and the youth A and B teams. I was in the B team. As soon as I put on the white Preston jersey and trained with and played against really, really good players it was like, 'I'm a footballer now already'.

"It was awesome just to be a part of that. It made me feel, 'This is it; this is what I have to do'. It was just amazing to be training with all those good players, most of whom were older and stronger than me. And the fitness level you had to reach was mind-blowing. To come from the local leagues and suddenly you are playing alongside and against professional people every week was unbelievably different."

Growing up and learning his trade, Alston loved watching his brother Alec in action and said he dreamed of emulating his career at Deepdale. It was a ground he often visited.

He always paid to watch the games and loved to stand behind the goals. His dad would be in the main stand.

"I was Preston through and through, and having an older brother playing for my club made me try to do what he did, even though as I said, our styles were rather different," he said.

Little did young Adrian know then that his career path was destined to take him to some 'exotic' places he would never have expected to go, let alone even heard of.

Alston was starting to make inroads into English football and learning something every day when he encountered a major problem—a common hurdle that would have destroyed any player with less resolve and hunger to become a pro.

"I could not even tell you who was the youth coach at Preston although [Willie] Cunningham [a Scottish international from the mid-50s] was one of our coaches and was always there at training and at our evening games," he recalled.

"I had to completely change my approach to the game because you had to step up by another 10 levels. You had to be better, stronger, faster and listen to what the coaches were saying rather than put your head down, arse up and do your own thing.

"Yet I still had this attitude that I wanted to do my own thing and obviously this did not get me to stay at Preston. I got different instructions in my formative years, which can be confusing. While my role at Preston was more tactical, when I was at Fleetwood later Kelly always encouraged me to take people on and be bold and creative.

"You see, Cunningham was a left fullback while Kelly was a right-sided midfielder and the messages I got from them were different.

"I wanted the ball all the time because I was in love with it and I would spend hour after hour juggling the ball outside on my own to hone my skills. In the 1960s there was only one match on television, a football show on the Saturday night and I often went to watch my brother Alec play, so I had a lot of free time (to practise)."

Alston unfortunately did not last long at Deepdale. After one season, he moved to non-league Fleetwood ... a step down perhaps, but with the promise of more first-team football.

However, his association with Preston did have a memorable moment when local hero Finney approached him one day to say hello.

"Finney knew I was Alec's brother. He of course had played alongside him before he retired and Alec left the club. I think he basically came over to meet 'Alec Alston's brother'. I just knew I was not looked upon as Adrian Alston so we had to change that, didn't we, I told myself. It was a nice moment nonetheless ... very special actually."

Fleetwood did not provide Alston with too much football mainly because a few months into the season, he was offered the opportunity to play in Australia. He would take it only after lengthy consideration. This was perfectly understandable, mind you, for someone who had never been abroad.

"I only played a handful of games for my next club Fleetwood, who had a strong side with several players from higher leagues. When Kelly hired me, he and other coaches at the club believed after a couple of games for the reserves, I should go straight into the first team. Which I did," he said.

But Alston's game based on speed and ball control was not really suited to the prevailing conditions. Pitches in England in winter in the '60s were not as immaculate as they are now, particularly those of the Premier League that look like carpets. They were often nothing less than a mud bath and on a rainy day you would have mud as high up as your knee.

Goodness knows how heavy the old leather balls must have felt. It could not have been too much fun for the finer and more technically endowed players. And Alston certainly was one such gifted player.

"That was when Kelly told me, 'We have to go to Australia'," Alston recalled. "He said he was taking on the coaching position at South Coast United after having led the club to a NSW grand final win over APIA Leichhardt in 1963."

In January 1968, Alston made the big and brave decision to quit English football to sign a short-term deal with South Coast.

Kelly's overtures had proven to be too hard to resist for a young man who was having trouble finding out where and how he fit into the game he loved so much.

Saying yes to Kelly and Australia was a gamble because Alston's trip to a faraway land was nothing less than a mysterious journey—like going on a blind date—despite his mentor's promises that playing in the top division in NSW on firm and dry (if rather bumpy) pitches would enhance his talents and make him a better player.

Australian football, to be fair, was not as highly regarded then as it is now.

The national team had never qualified for a World Cup.

In their only attempt to reach the finals, the poorly prepared Socceroos were thrashed 9–2 by supremely fit North Korea over two legs in neutral Cambodia. The so-called 'diddy men' were no pushovers though and went on to reach the quarter-finals of the 1966 World Cup tournament in England.

The only Australian player who had earned any degree of recognition and respect in Britain was Joe Marston. The Sydney-born defender was a mainstay at Preston in the first half of the 1950s and played in the losing FA Cup final side against West Brom in 1954.

So Alston would have had every reason to feel that an English footballer taking his boots to Australia made as much sense as a Brazilian surfer taking his boards to Alaska.

However, subsequent events would reward Kelly's wise judgement and Alston's raw courage.

Club football in Australia was limited to state competitions until a semi-professional national championship was launched in 1977. A fully professional national competition—the A-League—would come much later in 2005.

When Alston arrived in Australia, NSW had two divisions and South Coast were one of 12 clubs in the top tier.

The others were 1967 grand final winners St George Budapest, premiers APIA Leichhardt, Hakoah Eastern Suburbs, Pan Hellenic, Sydney Prague, South Sydney Croatia, Polonia North Side, Yugal, Canterbury-Marrickville, Melita Newtown and Manly-Warringah.

The second division also comprised 12 clubs.

South Coast were the only team from outside Sydney in both divisions.

Nearly all clubs were founded and supported by European migrants who had flocked to Australia at the end of World War II. The First Division league was therefore a competition that mirrored multicultural Australia to a tee. It would give the young import an instant insight into a cultural world that could not be any more removed from the one he was used to back home.

Alston would undergo a 'cultural evolution' in Australia.

Playing 'down under' would be an eye-opening exercise and all part of a learning process that would benefit him immensely over the years, particularly when he became a regular Socceroos' striker in the 1970s.

He said he left behind many beautiful memories of playing with his friends in the streets of Ribbleton before taking his first steps to becoming a footballer in and around the Preston area. Football then became the prime focus of his young life, and to a degree, some friendships had to take a back seat.

But Alston never forgot where he came from, even at the peak of his career when he would fulfil every child's dream of playing in the World Cup and, perhaps more significantly, become a professional in England's First Division.

"You didn't drift away because obviously you were still living in the same area, although I never used to drink or go to the pub and stuff like that. Those things would not happen," he said.

"However my move to Preston did really hit my friends because I was not playing in their league anymore. At the time my mates would have said, 'Ah well, he's playing in a new grade' and that's it. But none of them ever imagined that one day I would go on to play in the World Cup and be watched by millions on television or become a professional footballer in the highest division in England. Let alone both.

"I remained in contact with some of my local mates, of course. I had to admire and respect them because as fellow footballers they were part of why I became someone. Yet I was still me, you know. I never changed at all after I became a professional footballer, so I had no problem with my real friends and they had no problem with me."

So, was Alston the footballer and young man ready for the biggest challenge of his career and his life? It was, after all, something few players of his age would have been faced with.

You bet he was. "In my head, I was the best," he said.

On 26 January 1968—Australia Day—Alston boarded a Qantas flight from Heathrow in London bound for Sydney.

Australian football was about to get a new hero.

Chapter 3
Prawn cocktails, sun and surf

South Coast United 'jack-of-all-trades' Trevis Birch was getting anxious as he awaited the arrival of the English centre-forward who was contracted specifically to spearhead his club's drive for the NSW Division One title.

It was the morning of 28 January 1968. The Qantas plane that flew from New Delhi to Sydney had been landed for quite some time, but Birch could not locate the footballer who was supposed to be accompanied by the club's old hero, Kelly, who had agreed to coach the club for a second time.

Alston cut a forlorn figure as he wandered around at the arrivals hall at Sydney airport and was becoming rather nervous too.

That was when a stranger came up to him.

"It was club official, Trevis Birch. I will never forget my arrival in Sydney and his expression when he saw me," Alston recalled.

"I was hanging around and hanging around like a lost soul and finally this man, who was not a big bloke, came up to me and asked, 'Are you Adrian Alston?'

"I said 'Yes, I am'. I will never forget the look on his face when he realised that the big and tall English centre-forward he was expecting turned [out] to be just a boy. I was five foot seven and weighed about 65 kilos in those days. You could just tell that he was very disappointed."

Having made the all-important first contact and come to terms with his initial shock, Birch composed himself well enough to ask a second question: "Where is Jim?"

"It's a long story," Alston told him.

"Kelly picked me up from home in Preston and we got a cab to the station to catch a train for London. None of my family came to Heathrow Airport to see me off because a train ticket from Preston to London would have cost a fortune those days. So the goodbyes took place at home.

"The problem arose after we stayed overnight in Delhi, and Kelly, who was very frugal with money, put me up at a YMCA motel.

"The next morning when we returned to the airport to resume our journey to

Sydney, we discovered that Kelly was the only one booked on the flight. My name was just not on the list of passengers, maybe because I had not made up my mind about travelling 'til the last minute.

"It was difficult for the airline to get me on the plane and all they could do was put me on the next flight, which is when Kelly kindly offered to swap tickets.

"So I went on the first flight mainly because we knew Trev would be waiting for me at Mascot. Kelly was told he would have to travel a few hours later."

Having sorted that one out, Birch decided to kill the time until Kelly's arrival by giving the English import his first taste of Australia. Birch took him on a drive around Sydney on a hot and sunny day that could not have portrayed the city in a more attractive way.

"Since Kelly was arriving later in the day, Birch drove me around Sydney in his flash American car and I was able to see for the first time the Harbour Bridge, the Opera House, the harbour and some of the city's best parts," Alston remembered.

"I just went, 'Wow, bloody hell, this place is unbelievable'. I was not expecting such a big city because all I had heard about Australia in England was kangaroos, sheep, et cetera. I did not pay too much attention to what was being said on television because I was always out kicking a ball, and later as I grew older, I was hanging out with my girlfriend and I was never home before midnight. It was just a shock to my system to see such a beautiful city. A very pleasant shock, to be honest.

"Trev loved his cars and was delighted to show me around. He was a wonderful man really. Officially, he was secretary manager of the club, but in reality, he was the boss. He took me under his wing immediately and would become like a father figure to me. After I played a few games for my new club he told me, 'If you stay in Australia, you'll become an international player'. Just like that. I never forgot those words. He was the main reason I remained in Australia, actually."

But it was mainly thanks to Kelly's insistence that Alston had made the big decision to leave his family, his childhood sweetheart Doreen and his friends, and come to unknown Australia. "I took his word that I would do well in Australia with him as my mentor because Jimmy was an excellent coach. You could tell straight away from the quality of his training with the ball and everything else. He was an England B international after all, and he looked after himself very well health wise," he said.

So did young Alston have any serious reservations about opting out of his comfort zone?

No way. He of course had had some initial doubts, but he effectively saw life in the same way as he played his football: his only focus was on reaching his goals and if it meant taking a few risks or knocks along the way, so be it.

It was with this bold and cavalier attitude that Alston had flown halfway around the globe to take the next step in his fledgling career.

"I was just excited by the thought of just playing football on the other side of the world," he recalled.

"It was all about the game and it did not matter which country I was going to. All I had in my mind was playing full-time. I had to get a job while I was in England. I drove a truck once because you had to make a quid.

"I travelled to Sydney in my best suit. I did not take too many clothes with me because in them days I did not earn enough money for a big wardrobe. Besides, Kelly advised me about the type of clothes I would be wearing in Australia. He said I would be in shorts all the time and I started laughing. The last time I had worn shorts was when I was at school.

"Kelly also told me I was going to play for South Coast United in the First Division of NSW against some very strong teams and players, some of them Australian internationals. And besides that, I would face a lot of foreigners who were playing 'down under'. This prospect of testing myself at a higher level provided me with a huge thrill."

Having finally met up with Kelly at the airport, the three made their way to the Illawarra region that is famous for its surf and sandy beaches. This was to be Alston's idyllic home for about six to eight months, depending on whether South Coast made the end-of-season finals.

What transpired on Alston's first day left him nothing less than gobsmacked.

Kelly had booked him in at the YMCA in Fairy Meadow just outside Wollongong but he did not check in because it was time for lunch. Alston and Kelly were taken by a few club officials to a restaurant in the Thirroul area.

"I was asked if I would like a prawn cocktail for starters and I replied, 'No thanks, I don't drink' and everybody burst into laughter. They thought I was joking but I was quite serious," Alston said.

"When I was politely advised that prawns had nothing to do with alcohol and I realised they were different to the tiny shrimps I was used to back home, I ordered a cocktail before the main meal along with about 10 glasses of orange juice. I tell you, I could have had one of those prawn cocktails every day. They were so good.

"After lunch we went down to the ground in Woonona to watch the South Coast reserves play. It must have been a hundred degrees and we walked in there to be greeted by a few people who wanted to talk to me, among them some local journalists and photographers. They saw this whiter-than-white young bloke in a beige suit that was specially made for me by a Jewish tailor in Blackpool. We sat down to watch the game that had already started and at halftime Kelly said, 'Come on, let's go, let's get ready'. I said, 'What for?', to which he bluntly replied, 'You're on in the next game'.

"I just could not believe it. I was absolutely knackered. I had just flown 20,000 kilometres from Britain, had been in the country for only a few hours, had just come back from a big lunch and I was boiling up on a stinking hot day ... and they wanted me to play!

"Anyway, I went into the dressing room. Striker Max Tolson was not available that day for the pre-season game against Hakoah because he had not yet agreed terms with the club. The players just laughed at me because I was just pale white and they were all nicely tanned. It was the middle of summer, of course.

"So that is when I made my debut for the club ... and to cap off a rather memorable and eventful day I also scored a couple of goals. The first was a simple tap-in but the second was a pretty good strike from about 25 metres. After the game, delighted Trev said that I had done enough to make him change his mind about my size."

Alston had a pretty decent contract that was a far cry from the paltry wage he was getting at Fleetwood.

He was to be paid $60 a game for one season. The club even found him a cushy job at the instrument room at the nearby steelworks that earned him another $60 a week.

"This will do me," he said to himself.

"Later on in the season the club offered me a two-year deal which I accepted. Which of course meant I had to stay in Australia for another year and for the first time in my life, I was going to spend Christmas away from home. It just was too expensive to go to Britain and come back in the off-season. I was earning $60 a week and I could not afford the return fare that cost about $600. But I was playing football and I was happy enough doing that.

"The whole South Coast United committee were excellent and wonderful people to deal with. They looked after me very well and I could not speak highly enough of them.

"I had a return ticket to the UK as part of my deal with South Coast but I never got to use it."

Kelly had told Birch that Alston was to stay at the YMCA for a week or so after he first arrived until he sorted out his accommodation. He urged the official not to spoil him. Kelly wanted Alston to understand that his move was not going to be as easy as his first outing might have suggested, and that he would have to work hard to make the grade. He had to earn his wages, basically.

However, Birch knew almost immediately that the club was on a winner with its fresh recruit and he vowed to do everything in his power to make sure the player was happy in his new surroundings.

After his dream debut against Hakoah, Alston had dinner with several supporters at the nearby Woonona Bulli Soccer Club before finally going back to the YMCA for a well-earned sleep. It had been a momentous first day in Australia.

His stay at the modest motel would not last long.

Birch went over to the YMCA that evening to check if everything was okay with Alston and what he saw was a lonely young man sitting on his bed, thousands of kilometres from home.

"Trev must have felt my predicament because the next morning he came around to cheer me up by showing me the coverage I got in the papers and he invited me to his place for breakfast. His wife Priscilla cooked me steak and eggs. I would end up staying with the Birches for 10 months and having such a sumptuous breakfast nearly every morning. I think 'Cill' was trying to build me up. If Trev was like a father to me, she was indeed like a mother. My daughter Debbie's second name is in fact Priscilla, named after her."

Things were going smoothly and Kelly had every reason to be satisfied with Alston's baptism of fire in blistering hot Australia. He just knew that Alston and South Coast were a marriage made in heaven.

Kelly had been very successful in Australia with South Coast in the mid-1960s. After a long career in England, he wanted to play football 'down under' but Blackpool wanted a hefty transfer fee for him. He managed to come here only because our football association was banned from FIFA at the time due to its poaching practices.

"Kelly was like a god within the South Coast organisation and when he promised the club that I would be a success in Australia, they believed him. And so did I," Alston said.

The process of moving to Australia was smooth and uncomplicated by today's standards.

It is worth noting that Alston did not have a representative when he came to Australia.

In fact he would spend the rest of his career without the services of someone to look after his football-related affairs.

"Nobody, it was always just me. I never had an agent in my entire career," he said.

"I suppose that's probably why, along the way, I could have got better contracts everywhere. Of course I could.

"For example, (English striker) Rodney Marsh's manager who also looked after George Best once approached me a few years later while I was having a drink after a game at Tampa Bay Rowdies in America and asked me, 'Who's your agent?' I replied, 'I haven't got one'. He then asked me how long my contract was for. I told him it was for three years, to which he said, 'See me when your contract is up because you are losing a lot of money.'"

Chapter 4
Striker leaves his mark

Alston, the young Englishman who bravely undertook a long journey to the other side of the world to further his career, was looking forward to his debut season in Australia as the kickoff to the 1968 NSW Division One approached.

The Preston-born striker was busy trying to adjust to the local playing conditions and doing well in trial matches in South Coast United's colours.

Spirits were high and a sense of guarded optimism prevailed at the Woonona-based club.

With coach Kelly at the helm, South Coast were eager to give the 12-team championship a shake after finishing second last in the previous season.

South Coast did not have an overly impressive record in terms of trophies—they had won the grand final in 1963 and the premiership two years later under Kelly's leadership—but they nonetheless were a well- established club in the Illawarra region, south of Sydney.

To put things in perspective, they were by no means inferior in terms of popularity or respect to the main rugby league club in the area that was yet to be part of the Sydney premiership.

The first team trained in Woonona three times a week but Alston, who was living with the Birches in nearby Corrimal, was keen to impress in his first season and chose to practise by himself on three more nights to improve his skills and get used to the hard, bumpy grounds.

"I had an easy job at the steelworks but I quit after three or four months because I wanted to concentrate entirely on my football and make sure I helped my team in the best possible way," he said.

"On my own I used to practise my dribbling, shooting and so on.

"The club was always good to me. They were not the type of people to give you the $60 a week and say, 'Here's your pay, off you go'.

"They were much more than that … they wanted to make sure that I was happy with everything and that I was in need of nothing. To this day I am still grateful to them."

The 'red and blacks' played their home matches at the Ball's Paddock ground in Woonona, which has since made way for development.

It was a tiny venue that drew an average crowd of about 2,000 supporters, but it suited Alston beautifully. It reminded him of the little grounds in the north of England although 'the hill' concept was new to him.

"It was a small ground but what I liked about it was the fact the fans were so close to you that you could almost touch them," he recalled fondly.

"They drove us continuously and passionately which was great because you felt that whenever we attacked, they were joining us in trying to score."

Woonona was seen as a difficult ground and no team in the league relished a trip down to the south coast.

Things were going rather smoothly in the pre-season and Alston was relishing playing under the bright skies of an Aussie autumn and winter. "Sometimes you needed a pair of sunnies to play," he quipped.

Of course, he knew very well that the real thing was the quest for competition points in the championship that would start in April.

So it was rather disappointing, if not deflating, for Alston, his eager teammates and the expectant supporters that South Coast lost the first league match of the season.

They crashed to a 1-0 defeat against St George Budapest in Sydney but they made amends a week later by thrashing Canterbury-Marrickville 7-2 at home.

In no time, Alston, his future international teammate Tolson and winger Denis Patterson were showing signs that they would become a dangerous strike force in the league.

Alston in fact ended his first season as joint league top scorer with 12 goals from 22 matches. The other player was fellow Englishman and South Coast teammate, Ron McGarry.

The problem with 'Kelly's Gang', as the South Coast team were known, was their poor away form which could have been the main reason why they finished in seventh spot, 13 points behind competition winners Hakoah Eastern Suburbs.

"We loved playing at home, but in our away games we missed the special atmosphere generated in Woonona," he said. "We hardly ever replicated our home form on the road so, yes, this is probably why we finished mid-table.

"Another reason might have been Kelly's departure halfway into the season. He had an insurance business back home in England that he needed to attend to and unfortunately, he had to leave the club."

Assistant coach Jim Harris took over the reins for the rest of the season.

If Alston was somewhat disappointed with the outcome of his first sortie into Australian football, 1968 would become a high point in his personal life because he married his childhood sweetheart, Doreen. She had joined him in Australia a few weeks after his arrival.

"The Birches kindly put us up at their place in Corrimal and for a while I was sleeping on a mattress on the floor of their second bedroom," Alston said.

"After about seven months Doreen and I decided to move out and we got married in August. Tolson was my best man. We lived in Corrimal, which is a place I love to this very day.

"The people were kind to us—they still are—and made us feel at home. Doreen loved being in Australia."

Alston would find bliss on the playing field too.

The second season provided him and his teammates with a vastly different outcome because the club became stronger in key areas, not least in the centre-half position.

Big man Peter Wilson came to Australia from Middlesbrough in early 1969 as a right back but he soon became a pillar in the middle of South Coast's defence.

"Wilson was far more valuable to us in the middle of our defence than as a fullback," Alston explained.

"He was a great tackler and header of the ball, and centre-half was just a natural position for him. He was tidy on the ball too."

Wilson's influence on the side was such that Alston regarded him and striker Tolson as the team's key men. "They were the hardest players I faced in my first two years in Australia," he said.

"It was good that they were on my side because I hardly ever had to face them as opponents. They were tough as nails and hated losing … even during practice."

South Coast started their campaign in much the same way as they kicked off their previous season: badly. They lost the first game against Hakoah when a Ray Baartz double helped his side to a 2–1 win at Wentworth Park.

But they recovered well and strung together 14 wins, only losing two more times to win the 1969 premiership after a bitter tussle with St George and Hakoah.

Alston etched his name in the club's history books by scoring the goal that gave South Coast a crucial 1–1 draw against APIA at Lambert Park in the last match of the regular season.

"Lambert Park was always a hard ground to go to and a few fans–not a great deal obviously–came up to Sydney to support us," he recalled.

"They used to follow us around. That was really encouraging because it always makes a difference.

"I drove up to the game with Wilson. I still remember my goal. Socceroos' right back George Keith came across to tackle me as I was shooting but I was too quick for him and the ball went into the net to give us the draw that would earn us the premiership."

Harris's South Coast won the title by finishing a mere point ahead of the Saints and two more than Hakoah. But in NSW, the team finishing first past the post was not considered the champion. That honour fell to the winner of the grand final.

"Winning the premiership was a lovely occasion but it would have been nice to finish off with a home game in front of our loyal fans," he said.

"After the match, Wilson and I drove down to our club to celebrate and we were greeted by many delighted supporters. The place was packed. It was a very special moment and, needless to say, I did not pay for one single drink that night.

"Winning the league was a remarkable achievement. The two Sydney teams that challenged for the title were full of international players, while I was the only one at South Coast. Wilson and Tolson, you see, had yet to play for the Socceroos.

"It was the first 'championship' of my career. However, in hindsight, that league win was also a source of disappointment for me because of the mentality in Australian sport. In Australia Rules and rugby league, for example, it is all about winning the grand final and in soccer it is the same, so our feat of winning the title was seen in a different light.

"Even in my coaching career, I was more concerned about winning the league than the grand final. They call it the minor premiership here … but I tell you there is nothing minor in winning the premiership."

South Coast, St George, APIA and Hakoah finished in the top four and played out a round-robin finals' series.

However, finals football—which was (and still is) seen by traditionalists as a lottery—was not as rewarding for Alston's team.

South Coast would have reached the grand final with victory over APIA in the third and final match, but they crashed to a shock 7–2 defeat.

APIA went on to beat the Saints 3–2 in the decider.

Despite South Coast's finals' debacle, Alston's exploits at the 'pointy end' of the team were not overlooked. Inevitably, they brought him to the attention of state and national selectors.

In May 1969—soon after the start of his second season in Australia—he was selected to play for NSW against New Caledonia.

Two months later, he went one better by being named in an Australia squad for a friendly international match against Greece.

Alston knew that this was a golden opportunity to take the next step in his career. He gave it everything at training, scoring five times for the 'second' team against the 'first' team in a practice match leading up to the game.

Alston's five-star performance must have convinced coach Joe Vlasits that he deserved to be in the starting line-up.

"I was not expecting to start when I joined the squad and when 'Uncle Joe' was reading out the line-up just before the match, there was no mention of my name until it came up last because I was on the left wing at No. 11," Alston said.

"I was so glad. The coach then said to me in his heavy accent, 'Aaadriaan, how do you feel?' To which I replied, deadpan, 'I suppose that's the end of my English career'.

"All the players at first stayed silent but after a while they all burst into laughter. It was just me being cocky as usual."

Alston duly started and helped Australia to a 1–0 victory in front of a 30,000-plus crowd at the Sydney Cricket Ground. The kid from Preston had never played in front of so many spectators.

The striker was in very good company that day. Some of the players who took part in the match such as Manfred Schaefer, John Watkiss, Johnny Warren, Atti Abonyi and Baartz either were or would become household names within Australia's football fraternity.

"The selection to play for my new country certainly vindicated my decision to leave England and come to Australia," he said.

"I said, 'Wow' … I'm an international player'."

Happy days.

Chapter 5
Dream call-up for Australia

Young Alston had become a revelation and a local hero after his first season in Australian football with South Coast in 1968.

In a short time, the English forward had established himself as one of the finest and most feared strikers in NSW's First Division even though his new club finished in the lower half of the table.

His 12 goals for the club did not go unnoticed or unrewarded and his selection to play for NSW in 1969 did not surprise anybody. It was seen as a natural progression for someone who had found a new dimension to his game away from the boggy fields of northern England.

But the natural goalscorer received the shock of his life in mid-1969 when—with his second season in full swing—his club informed him that he had been picked in Australia's train-on squad for a three-match series against Greece.

Alston was quite happy to be regarded merely as an interstate player at that stage of his young career but the prospect of turning out for the Australian team in a full international match blew him away.

He just did not see the call-up coming. Not so soon after setting foot in the country, anyway.

"I could not even dream of getting picked for the Australian national team," he recalled.

"After my first season I was selected for NSW but it never entered my mind that I could be picked for the green and gold. Not for one second.

"Playing for NSW is probably what got me into the national squad. We played Victoria and I scored a couple of goals but I still had to pinch myself when the national call came.

"I was young and still learning and I just did not see myself as an international footballer. I was glad to play for NSW and I thought to myself, *That's it*. Australia had many good attacking players at the time like Abonyi, Warren and Baartz, and I was just incredibly proud of the prospect of playing with those guys.

"When my club got the call from the federation and learning that I was named in the train-on squad, it did not really hit me until the day I got to meet the boys up in Sydney. You can imagine how surprised I was to start the match.

"The squad was mainly from NSW, with one or two players from Victoria.

"In my first season in Australia I was just concentrating on my club football. Those days it was all about Sydney and there existed an 'us versus them' mentality. We just felt—or rather I felt—we were a bit separate from them and you had more to prove on the south coast. Basically, you had to do a lot more to get selected in the national squad if you were a south coast player.

"The selectors must have seen something in me—which was nice—but it still took me a year to establish myself in the national set-up.

"I wrote a letter to my dad to tell him the good news but I think my wife Doreen might have sent him a telegram. He obviously was over the moon."

Experienced Ron Corry was in goal when Alston introduced himself to international football in the first match against the Greeks in front of a big crowd in Sydney to become the 205th Socceroo.

He said he knew straight away that Alston would become a key man in Australia's quest to reach the 1970 World Cup in Mexico.

"He was always a brash and fully confident young man and that's how he played his football,' Corry remembered.

"You could tell even then that he was going to be a good player because he obviously had the skill and he had no fear of anyone. His biggest fear was singing on the bus.

"He was playing regularly for a strong South Coast side and scoring every week and he was up there with our best strikers like Warren, Baartz and Abonyi."

Australia had played only three international matches since Alston arrived in the country in early 1968 before they took on the Greeks.

Vlasits had overseen a three-match series with Japan that took place in autumn, a few weeks after the Englishman's arrival.

Alston never got to watch any of those three international matches so the Australian team would have been as familiar to him as one from outer space.

"I had never seen the national team play before I made my debut in July 1969 and I knew very little about 'Uncle Joe'," he admitted.

"Needless to say, I had no idea what style of football the team played. I was picked to be the target man but it was hard to fit in, to be honest.

"I had a very ordinary half of football. It was just difficult against a very strong Greek team. I did not see much of the ball and the fact that I hardly knew the players I was playing with did not help.

"Vlasits gave me 45 minutes and he was good to me afterwards. He put his arm around me and assured me everything would be okay. 'You've done pretty well to shoot up the ladder in one season … you have a long career ahead of you and you will be a star for Australia in years to come,' he promised me."

Eligibility rules in Australia were different in the 1960s and a player was allowed to don the green and gold jersey even though he was British.

"It was only after we went to South Korea for the first phase of qualifying for the 1970 World Cup that I received my Australian passport," he recalled.

"The Koreans made some noises about me and Scotland-born Tommy McColl not being 'proper' Australians and travelling on British passports, and our federation had to act fast. On our return home, we were given a letter from the Queen informing us that we had become naturalised Australians. I got my passport and it is the only one I have used since. I am not a dual citizen … I am Australian."

But despite his strong club form, Alston was overlooked for the first phase of World Cup qualifying.

The Australians had been comprehensively beaten by stronger and fitter North Korea in a playoff for the 1966 World Cup and this time they were keen to go one better.

They were drawn to play South Korea and Japan in a round-robin in Seoul, with the winners to play an African team and ultimately Israel for the right to play in the finals in Mexico.

Australia won the group with two wins and two draws although they had to survive a few anxious moments in their final match against the Koreans in front of a big and boisterous crowd in Seoul.

"I watched the four matches on the bench, which was okay. I was not too disappointed and it was not hard to watch the boys go around. Football never made me overly nervous anyway and as coach Rale Rasic would tell me later, my bombastic attitude and joking around might have compensated for any nerves I could have had."

Rhodesia, which is now Zimbabwe, became Africa's sole contestant for a place in the finals in Mexico after the rest of the continent withdrew en bloc in protest. The country was racially divided with a tiny white minority holding political and economic power since it gained independence from Britain in 1965.

Vlasits's team was ordered by FIFA to play Rhodesia over two legs in neutral Mozambique for the right to face the Israelis.

That was some neutral and fair venue. It was like Sydney playing Perth in 'neutral' Wollongong or Fremantle!

"It was a horrible trip," Alston remembered. "We arrived in Johannesburg from Sydney from where we were supposed to fly to Mozambique's capital city, Laurenco Marques (now Maputo). The final leg of the trip got disrupted when three of the squad members including myself were left behind because there were not enough seats on the plane to fit us all in.

"So we three players and an Australian Soccer Federation official were forced to arrive a day later. I was convinced Vlasits had left me behind in South Africa because he did not intend to use me in the first match.

"We rejoined the group in a wonderful hotel in the nicer part of the city and in no time we went to the Salazar Stadium for a training run on the eve of the match.

"When we arrived at the ground it was dark and as soon as they switched on the floodlights we were greeted by the extraordinary spectacle of a million frogs that scattered and took off to the surrounding areas.

"The Rhodesians were tougher to beat than expected. We got a 1–1 draw in the first match but I was not picked for the second match that ended 0–0.

"We had only ourselves to blame for not settling the tie after wasting several scoring chances in both matches, so we had to stay in Mozambique for two more days to take part in a decider which we eventually won 3–1.

"The unplanned decider meant that we had two fewer days to prepare for our date with the Israelis, which was now only five days away.

"Having said that, staying in Laurenco Marques and playing World Cup qualifiers [was] a great experience. It was a big thing for me. Twenty months earlier I was playing for non-league Fleetwood!

"Having to play a third match was seen as a pain but the bottom line was that our dream of playing in a World Cup was still intact … the thing is I remember very little about those three matches. Getting old may have something to do with this.

"What I do remember however is the return journey home which was even more horrendous than the first trip.

"We flew from Laurenco Marques to Johannesburg, then on to Luanda in Angola. We were not allowed to step off the plane (because it was too dangerous to do so due to political tensions) before we resumed our journey to Lisbon, from where we got on another flight to Rome. From Italy we then flew to Athens before boarding yet another plane for Tel Aviv, arriving less than 24 hours before we had to face Israel at the notorious Ramat Gan Stadium.

"We were absolutely knackered. I wish we had the luxury of charter fights with on-board masseurs that some Socceroos squads have these days.

"But if the truth be told, our failure to beat the modest Rhodesians over two matches came back to bite us."

The trip from Mozambique to Tel Aviv had taken no less than 36 hours. It was even more physically and emotionally draining than the onward journey from Australia.

"After beating the Rhodesians, we seemed to spend all the time squashed in a plane or at an airport waiting for a flight. Absolutely ridiculous. And for one who hates flying like myself, it was even more dreadful," he said.

"Over the years, we would spend so much time in the air and in different beds and hotels that our sleeping patterns were always interrupted. For a long time I spent more time with my teammates than with my wife. Looking back, you ask yourself, 'How did we manage to do that?'"

It was indeed a measure of the Australians' desire, drive and determination to succeed that they emerged from an impossible assignment against Israel with a narrow 1-0 defeat, thanks largely to a penalty save from goalkeeper Corry.

Alston did not play in Tel Aviv and was yearning for a crack at captain Mordechai Spiegler's side in the return match in Sydney 10 days later, but he was again overlooked.

"We gave it our best shot against a very talented team and could have won the game—make that we should have won—but all we could manage was a 1-1 draw and we were therefore eliminated at the very last hurdle," he recalled.

Israel went on to leave a very favourable impression at the finals in Mexico, even drawing with Sweden and eventual finalists.

The Australians' cause was not helped by their cash-strapped federation's controversial decision to let the players go home after returning from Israel instead of keeping them together to prepare for the return match in Sydney.

It was clearly a money-saving exercise. It was not the first time and would not be the last time that the game's authorities in Australia made a business decision instead of a football decision.

"They always did that, making it difficult at the time for all of us to start thinking as professionals," Alston said.

"Playing in a pressure-cooker atmosphere in Israel, it really went into my head that I desperately wanted international football in my veins and to play against the best teams in the biggest events. But without the federation's full support, we had little chance.

"Israel flew to Sydney with us but while we were sent home they went straight into camp to plot our downfall. It was a typical situation because that sort of thing happened time after time after time.

"Vlasits did not want to rock the boat. No way would Rasic have accepted that ridiculous scenario … he would have put his foot down.

"Don't get me wrong. I was very proud and privileged to play for my adopted country but in hindsight we could have done things a lot better. The preparation was never as it should have been and that was the frustrating part.

"We were part-timers and many of us had given everything—even given up their job—to follow our dream of playing in the World Cup.

"I lost my job to play for Australia in that 1970 campaign and over the years I would lose a total of four jobs. How can you get the time off to be running off to Sydney and be whisked away to other countries all the time? Employers were not happy with you not turning up for work and you were left with no other alternative but to quit.

"To rub salt into our wounds, we were paid the princely sum of $15 each for our efforts to get to the World Cup. It was a shocking insult."

Yet despite the disappointment and frustration of a failed campaign, Alston had seen enough of the special atmosphere surrounding World Cup qualification that he desperately wanted to be part of it in the future. He vowed to keep fighting to realise his ambition.

His time would come.

Chapter 6
Rapid rise woos Arok, Rasic

The late Frank Arok, who coached the Socceroos for six tempestuous years in the 1980s, knew a good player when he saw one.

And when the then St George coach was watching Alston in action in person during training for NSW in late 1969, he knew immediately that the striker with a fast-growing reputation was the man who could bring trophies to the ambitious, Sydney-based club.

Alston had just helped South Coast to the NSW First Division premiership and it was seen as only a matter of time before the more affluent clubs from Sydney would pounce on the young Englishman who had made his international debut that same year.

Arok had a hugely talented side that was led up front by Warren and Abonyi, and at the back by Schaefer. All three were star internationals. Top goalkeeper Jim Fraser was in the national squad too.

But the coach needed another quality striker who would put the icing on the Saints' cake and give the club its second league title in its history.

"Frank came after me massively because his club was expected to be as successful as the other big clubs in Sydney," Alston said.

"At NSW training one night, Frank was on the sidelines—he came there a few times—and kept yelling at Warren, urging him to invite me to join the Saints.

"Warren at the time was captain of St George, NSW and Australia, so he exerted a lot of influence. We also got to know each other very well.

"Arok knew I was under contract with South Coast, so he was not prepared to approach me directly to avoid any poaching accusations.

"I was quite flattered but then again I was always pretty confident in my own ability, so I saw no reason not to think about it.

"I was really happy at South Coast because the club was my home and they always treated me well. But Warren's direct approach was certainly tempting and I spoke to [club boss] Birch about it.

"I knew for a fact that Tolson, for example, was on much more money than myself, and deservedly so to be fair, because he was an excellent player for a number of years.

"So when the Saints offered me $100 a week compared with the $60 I was getting at South Coast, Trev and I had a talk about it and a transfer fee of $5,000 was agreed to by the two clubs. It was a hell of a lot of money for a transfer [in] those days.

"I signed for three years and I went with Birch's blessing but he did admit he was sad to see me go. So much so that he insisted on having a clause in my contract that stipulated South Coast could buy me back at the end of my deal with the Saints for the same amount of money." The Bosman ruling (players being free to move to a new club at the end of their contract without incurring a transfer fee) was light years away back then.

St George were among the finest teams in Australia in the early 1970s and Alston's acquisition made them formidable, if not unbeatable.

"From the start, Arok explained to me his philosophy and what he was trying to achieve," Alston said.

"He already had an excellent side but he just kept missing out on the honours. He said to me, 'You're the missing link for us and things will happen'. And they certainly did because at one stage we held all the trophies available in NSW football.

"He was an excellent coach and a top person too, one of the very best I ever worked with."

Alston was the type of footballer with such a high level of self-belief that he never let himself be overawed by the fact that he was moving from "little South Coast United" to a famous club that was crammed with international players.

He realised all along he would be in the limelight and his game would come under greater scrutiny, but that was never an issue for him.

"St George signed me to fix them up, so I did not feel I had to step up and I was glad to note that I was getting twice as much ball with the Saints as I used to get at South Coast," he explained.

"We were a far more attacking team which of course made us a far more superior team in the offensive sense.

"Playing for a club like St George was never going to be easy, but it was great to play alongside such genuine stars as Warren and Abonyi.

"Atti incidentally would give me the nickname 'Noddy' during a practice session with the national team. He was crossing balls from the wing and kept calling 'Noddy, Noddy' for me to jump and head towards goal. And it stuck.

"St George made me a better player I'd say, because I had more of the ball and that gave me more opportunities to show what I could do."

What about expectations? Did he feel he and his new teammates were under more pressure to succeed than he was with South Coast?

"Of course, you had to win and we had to win well," he recalled.

"We had to get trophies and do it in style, for sure, but pressure never got to me.

In fact, I probably thrived on it.

"I thoroughly enjoyed my three years with St George, which was a wonderful club with helpful people. I was close with a certain Emre Nagy, one of the directors who gave me a job at his printery and effectively made me his chauffeur. I used to drive him to and from the city for lunch with his Hungarian friends and most days he then would tell me to 'go home and get ready for training'."

A few months into Alston's stint with the Saints, a change in the national team's hierarchy would have a significant effect on his career.

Rasic took over the reins of the team in green and gold from Vlasits in mid-1970. He immediately mapped out a series of international matches and tours abroad to get the team in the best possible shape and frame of mind for the forthcoming qualifiers for the 1974 World Cup.

"I had big plans and, as usual, I was not going to compromise on anything," Rasic said in his book *The Rale Rasic Story*. "For me it was all about the squad and giving it the best possible chance to succeed. There would be no shortcuts, no skimping and no excuses. It was my way or forget it."

Alston was never able to command a regular spot in Vlasits's team after making his debut against Greece in early 1969, but he played twice for 'Uncle Joe' on his last national team assignment in April 1970.

Australia was invited to take part in a so-called Friendship Cup in Saigon (now Ho Chi Minh City) that was designed to boost Vietnamese morale in the midst of the Vietnam War.

In the semi-finals, Alston scored a first-half hat-trick to help Australia to a comfortable 6–2 win over a Hong Kong selection that played under the name of their sponsors, Kowloon Bus Company.

In the final, Alston was on the mark again in Australia's 1–0 victory over the South Vietnamese Army the following day.

These two matches are classified as B internationals, so Alston's four goals unfortunately did not count in his international goals tally.

"It is a bit annoying actually. The three goals I scored against Hong Kong don't seem to count as international goals even though the team we faced was the national side," Alston protested.

There are some grey areas in Australia's football history when it comes to A or B internationals.

Rasic soon made it clear that the 'English' striker was one of several key men in the team's quest to reach the finals in West Germany.

Ruthless Rasic would change the course of Australia's football history and establish Alston as a top international striker and a target of several European clubs.

Rasic also replaced Arok at St George in 1971 before moving to Marconi a year later, so for the three-year period leading up to the World Cup he had several of his Socceroos' 'probables' at his disposal at club level too.

In their first tour abroad in 1970, Rasic's team beat Israel 1–0 in Tel Aviv and Greece 3–1 in Athens, and they lost 3–0 to Mexico in Mexico City. They also played many matches against club and representative sides, including Luton and Manchester City.

Two years later, the national team players were on the road again. They beat Indonesia 4–1 and New Zealand 3–1 in Jakarta, South Vietnam 1–0 in Saigon, drew with South Korea 1–1 and beat them 2–0 in Seoul, and overcame the Philippines 6–0 in Manila.

As anyone who has travelled abroad would know, waiting for a delayed flight in an airport is not exactly an enjoyable exercise. Representative football players have had plenty of those experiences over the years. Sometimes the larrikin element within the group came to the rescue.

"One day we were on our way home and stuck in an Asian airport—it might have been Hong Kong—due to a delay and we were all bored to death," Alston said.

"A couple of the boys went to buy little toys for their kids. They had these little dogs with a battery that made them jump forward and bark. They would go forward three steps, sit up, bark and do a bit of a somersault, so we thought we'd lift our spirits by having a 'dog race'. The boys were putting in five dollars here, five dollars there and you should have seen the crowd at the airport watching these crazy Aussies have fun. The scene was unbelievable. It was hilarious. We could have caused a security alert."

In between those two foreign forays that showed very clearly that the team was becoming a force to be reckoned with, Australia faced Israel three more times in a home series in 1971.

What must have pleased Alston no end was the fact that he had played in all 12 matches in the three years since Rasic took over and he was now seen as an automatic choice in the side that had acquired a nickname.

Sydney journalist Tony Horstead started calling the national team the 'Socceroos'—exactly when this happened exactly is not clear—and the moniker stuck.

On one occasion—the first of the three internationals with Israel in Brisbane—Alston was asked to play at left back because Rasic did not have enough defenders.

Alston at that point asked Rasic, "Hey, boss, am I allowed to score from fullback?" and he duly obliged by scoring a late goal that gave the Australians a 2–2 draw.

"Rasic's appointment with the Socceroos and Saints was the best thing that could ever happen to me," Alston said.

"He knew what I could do after working with me every week at St George. And very soon I felt confident that I was his main striker for club and country.

"Rasic was a footballing intellectual who left nothing to chance in his drive to make us successful. What he was trying to do was put us under intense pressure so that we could handle anything when it came to the real thing.

"It was jump on a plane, get to a hotel, train, play and get back on a plane, and so on. And we did this over and over again.

"And he wanted us to live together and do everything together. One of the tours went for something like 11 weeks, so you just had to pack in your job. I never had a good attitude for work anyway but financially it would have been better to keep working and playing.

"He created every situation we could possibly face in our qualifying campaign and made sure we were well equipped to handle it when it mattered. He used to tell us, 'It does not matter what's happening around us … we are going to succeed'."

Alston also had an opportunity to share a playing field with Brazilian World Cup hero Pelé when Australia drew 2–2 with Santos in a tour match in Sydney in June 1971.

Pelé was at the peak of his popularity. A year earlier he had helped a magnificent Brazil side win the World Cup in Mexico amid widespread acclaim.

Wherever 'O Rei' (The King) played, big crowds flocked to watch him in action.

So was Alston overawed by Pelé's presence that drew 32,000 fans to the Sydney Sports Ground?

"Look, I am not pretending to be a superstar but it never bothered me to play against the superstars," he said.

"I'm not kidding myself … I was not the best player in the world but I had enough ability to play against them at international level. There is no point in feeling inferior. You just can't do that because you become half the player you are the moment you start respecting your opponent too much. You might as well not walk out the door.

"Incidentally, I played against Pelé three times altogether. The other two occasions were in America when I played for Tampa Bay Rowdies against his New York Cosmos in 1978. We beat them once."

Alston's first son (also Adrian), who was born four months earlier in February 1971, was one of the spectators at the Sydney match.

"My wife Doreen brought him to the game so he could have a first glimpse of his footballer father, but I must have played poorly because he slept all through the game," Alston quipped.

He regards his stint with the Saints as one of the most enjoyable of his career.

In his first year, Alston helped the Saints reach the grand final but they lost to Yugal Ryde 4–0. However, in his second year—with Rasic in charge of the team—they made amends by winning the championship with a 3–2 victory over Western Suburbs.

In 1972, the Saints won the premiership to cap a highly successful period for the club and for Alston personally. They had every reason to feel satisfied with the handsome return from their investment in Alston.

"The Saints went from not winning much to winning virtually everything," he said.

Alston of course revisited the south coast as an opponent several times during his stint with the Saints and he is pleased to say he was always treated respectfully by the Illawarra fans who once adored him.

"South Coast United, particularly the Birches, were like a family to me, so it felt a bit weird to be there as an away player," he recalled.

"There was never any problem with the fans because I always did the right thing by the club and I never had any arguments or hassles with them. They understood my position and they also appreciated the fact that my move made me a regular international player."

The Saints' success was not limited to NSW. In late 1971, they travelled to Tokyo to take part in a four-team tournament involving Japan's national team (Japan B) and Danish champions, Frem Copenhagen.

And this is when Alston the footballer became a ring-in doctor.

"Abonyi was trod on in the first match of the tournament and one of his big toes became black with all the blood underneath the nail, so he was unlikely to get any more action in Japan," he explained.

"I had seen our team doctor treat a similar injury by slowly drilling a hole in the middle of the toe, using a scalpel and drawing out the blood.

"So I told Atti, 'I'll fix it, mate'. I got a needle, burnt its point with a cigarette lighter to disinfect it, and I slowly made a hole and drew out the blood from the toe. But it worked so well it went right through to the flesh.

"Atti was able to play again in the event although the toe was sore … and guess what, he later discovered that it was broken."

The Saints won the round-robin event with two wins and a draw. Alston was named man of the series. His footballing reputation was spreading abroad.

But his reputation as a comedian went up a notch or two a few hours after the final match.

As winners of the tournament, St George were presented with a trophy and each member of the winning team was given a bouquet of flowers.

"We were in our tracksuits and we were driven to our plush hotel called the Akasaka Prince to find out that in the gardens, a very formal Japanese wedding with about 400 guests was in full swing," Alston said.

"We were standing outside the garden and having a look when I walked right through the crowd and presented my bouquet of flowers to the bride and groom.

"They were obviously shocked but they politely bowed to me and as I walked off to rejoin my teammates, I had 400 people bowing to me and I thought to myself, *What a dickhead.* But it turned out okay actually."

Chapter 7
All eyes on the 1974 World Cup

Alston and the rest of the Socceroos team were supremely confident that the experience gained and lessons learnt during the failed 1970 World Cup campaign would serve them in good stead in the qualifying rounds of the 1974 tournament.

The 10th world championship of football was to be held in West Germany and Rasic and his boys were determined to leave no stone unturned in a bid to reach the promised land, a place where no Australians had ever been.

However, before Alston could even think about what was ahead of him and his teammates in terms of international football, he had a little question about his club future to sort out.

His three years with St George were up at the end of 1972 and South Coast were keen on exercising a clause in his contract that allowed them to buy him back for the same price ($5,000) that they had sought and obtained for his original transfer at the end of the 1969 season.

The South Coast club, which had been taken over by a motor vehicle franchise and renamed Safeway United at the end of 1972, offered Alston a lucrative deal that included a block of land in Corrimal (north of Wollongong). The Socceroos' striker took the opportunity to return to a familiar place that was close to his wife Doreen's heart. He loved the spot too.

His immediate club situation sorted, Alston was looking forward to the first World Cup qualifying phase that comprised a round-robin against Iraq, New Zealand and Indonesia. He was by now an established player in Rasic's team and he would play every minute of all six matches.

"We had a strong, balanced and experienced squad with no bad players," Alston recalled.

"Most of us had gone through the ups and downs of the previous campaign together and we were confident that we had reached a stage where we could take on any adversary and deal with any curveball that was thrown at us.

"Even though we were part-timers, we were training and preparing like full-time professionals. We had gone to some difficult places in our travels abroad and we developed a high level of togetherness and fearlessness.

"Worldwide, Iraq were the heavy favourites to qualify from the group and we were not expected to survive but, I tell you, that was not how we saw it in our minds. After we got a draw in New Zealand, I scored two goals in a 3–1 victory over the Iraqis in Sydney that set us up very nicely.

"All six matches were difficult except for our last fixture versus Indonesia which we won 6–0, but our strong belief helped us win the section, one point ahead of Iraq."

Alston cannot speak highly enough of the role Rasic played in Australia's success in the first qualifying phase.

Rasic knew his football like the back of his hand and, perhaps more significantly, he was an excellent man manager who is still respected and loved by all the surviving Socceroos' players who were lucky enough to cross paths with him.

The 'boss' had a strong personality; he knew what he wanted and how to get it. And he was not the sort of coach who would kowtow to officials, especially when the interests and welfare of his players were concerned.

"Rale gave up a lot to give us the best possible chance to realise our dreams," Alston said.

"And for him, his players always came first. Our preparation was excellent and we knew all along that our coach would back us all the way, but we never realised until later the level of sacrifice he made for us players.

"We sacrificed a lot too ... family-wise, business-wise, jobs-wise ... everything had to be put on hold during the entire campaign."

Safeway United obviously would not have been too happy to see their key players Alston, Max Tolson and Peter Wilson (who had all returned to the south coast) go away almost every other month on national team duty during their NSW Division One season.

Safeway had a somewhat disrupted 1973 and finished the season mid-table but Alston believes that there are considerable advantages for clubs that have international players on their books.

"It's just the way it is. I know international call-ups are hard on clubs but they also have to realise that when you are an international footballer, you can offer your club 10 times more than you would if you were not. It comes from the experience you gain from playing at a higher level and which you bring to the club," he explained.

"It also helps the club in terms of drawing fans to their games and attracting advertising and corporate support to be able to boast a number of international players."

Australia's opponents in the next phase of World Cup qualifying were Iran. In the first leg in Sydney in August of 1973, the Socceroos played one of the best matches of their campaign to emerge 3–0 winners with goals from Alston, Abonyi and Wilson.

Most pundits and supporters believed that the Socceroos had done enough to seal a place in a final playoff after such a comprehensive victory. No way could the Iranians overturn such a heavy deficit, it was thought.

Well, events in Tehran a week later showed that there was to be no easy passage for the Australians.

A fanatical crowd of 120,000 turned the notorious Azadi Stadium into a cauldron of noise and passion. The home fans were baying for blood … Aussie blood.

The Socceroos were somewhat shaken by such a hostile atmosphere and before they knew it, they had fallen behind to a dubious penalty.

The Iranians continued to attack and after half an hour they scored a second goal.

The Socceroos were clearly in big trouble and this is when Rasic made a substitution that could have made the difference between progression and elimination. He chose to replace the isolated and ineffective Alston at the pointy end of the attack with renowned impact player Tolson in a move designed to stem the Iranians' initiative.

Tolson was sitting next to Rasic on the bench during the first half and he could tell that the coach's impassive exterior was just a facade. "He was burning inside, I can tell you, and at the end of the first half he grabbed me forcefully by my hair and told me 'warm up'," Tolson told *The World Game* website.

The move worked a treat because Iran was somewhat put off by Tolson's raw aggression. The fighting Tolson, whom Rasic described as the best target man he had ever worked with, made his presence felt and gradually relieved the pressure on the Socceroos' defence by giving the Iranians something more to think about in their own half.

The score remained unchanged and it allowed the Australians to squeeze through 3-2 on aggregate. It was a close shave for the Socceroos but what mattered most was the fact that the World Cup was getting closer and closer.

"It was the hardest match in our whole campaign, no doubt," Alston said.

"Iran were on fire and they put us under intense pressure from the kickoff, so very soon we had our backs to the wall. But even when we went two down, we never for a moment thought we were gone. We always played to the end.

"I was on my own up front in Tehran and I had a very, very ordinary game. It was difficult to get the ball and when I did get it, I was swamped and kicked all the time. The referee must have been intimidated by the hostile crowd and gave us absolutely nothing, but he had no hesitation in giving them a dodgy penalty.

"I always hated being replaced but Rasic did the right thing by taking me off at halftime. He put Max on and he typically battled away as he was a fearless type of player and he did a great job for us. He had a top second half and fought for everything.

"It was an inspired substitution but that was typical Rasic … he had to do his job and he did it. The 'boss' was never afraid to make early changes, even if they might have appeared to be too early. The bugger used to replace me soon after I scored when I'm chasing a second."

Rasic, who is one of Alston's greatest admirers, once said half-jokingly that Alston sometimes got too cocky after scoring a goal and needed to be brought down to earth by taking him off.

Alston admits that he disliked the lone striker's job he was often given in Australia's away matches.

Australia usually played with at least two out-and-out strikers when they played at home or when they needed a win, but away matches were different. Caution became the norm.

"Being a striker is already a difficult job because even if you have two or three forwards, you are still outnumbered by the opposition's defence," he explained.

"So you can imagine how [much] harder it is when you are the only one up front and you have to deal with a stopper *and* usually a sweeper. When you get the ball, you must control it and hang on to the bloody thing until the support arrives. And if your team is playing defensively, it's a long, long way for the defenders and midfielders to come up to help you.

"Having said that, we had two very strong overlapping fullbacks in Doug Utjesenovic and Col Curran who could provide dangerous crosses.

"The best times I had in the Socceroos' jersey were in matches at home when we usually went for broke and I had a player or two beside me. That's when I felt most comfortable."

After beating the dangerous Iranians, Australia's players knew they were within touching distance of the World Cup and the team standing between them and a spot in the finals was going to be South Korea.

The tie was to take place over two legs in Sydney and Seoul and for the first time the Australians were genuinely confident that this was going to be the year they broke the World Cup drought. If they could survive Tehran, they would handle anything, right?

The Socceroos had enough chances to win the first leg but could not go past a 0–0 draw at the Sports Ground in front of a supportive crowd of 32,000.

And when the Koreans jumped to a 2–0 lead inside 30 minutes in the return a week later, many supporters in Australia feared the Socceroos' dream was about to be crushed at the last hurdle, the same as it was four years earlier by Israel.

But a goal from striker Branko Buljevic soon after the Koreans' second gave the Socceroos renewed hope. Ray Baartz scored an equaliser a few minutes after the start of the second half to take the match to a decider in Hong Kong.

Rasic had already won a crucial battle with the Koreans by forcing FIFA to bring forward the date of the decider (should it be needed) from five to three days later. He reasoned that since the Australians were physically and mentally stronger than the

Koreans, they would handle the turnaround much better than their adversaries.

It would turn out to be yet another master stroke from an old fox that got the seal of approval from the entire squad simply because they were used to quick turnarounds and recoveries. They had been doing it for years.

"Rale was spot on," Alston said. "Mentally we were stronger because he made us that way since he took over three years earlier. We wanted to get on with it and win the tie. Playing three days later was no big deal for us."

The epic decider was settled when midfielder Jimmy Mackay hit a screamer from outside the penalty area soon after Alston had replaced Abonyi to give Australia a historic 1–0 victory.

"It was a tense and hard-fought match, and we would have been able to relax a bit more towards the end had a shot of mine gone in rather than scrape the bar from a similar distance a few minutes after Mackay's wonder strike," Alston recalled.

"But hey, what a goal to take us to the World Cup."

Alston and his mates were promised half of the prize money that the Australian federation would receive for reaching the World Cup finals. So the jubilant players decided to celebrate their finest hour by using some of the promised money that same night.

Some of the players, Alston included, asked for an advance on the bonus but they ended up spending more than they could afford because they did not figure that after taxes and whatnot, the sum received would be much smaller than they anticipated.

"I spent a lot of money that night buying drinks and presents but at the end of the whole exercise I was in debt because the size of the bonus was considerably smaller," he said.

"But nobody really cared … we were going to the World Cup!"

The intrepid Socceroos returned to Australia to a hero's welcome and could afford to put their feet up over Christmas in anticipation of their great World Cup adventure. They would play tough cookies East Germany, Cup favourites West Germany and feisty Chile.

After a well-deserved rest in the festive period, Rasic and his men got down to business and played two trial matches against the touring Ferencvaros of Hungary before taking on Uruguay in a two-match series in April.

The two national teams drew 0–0 in the first match in Melbourne and Australia won the second match 2–0 in Sydney.

The result meant very little in the general scheme of things, but the event became one of the saddest and most heartbreaking moments in Australian football history because it marked the end of Baartz's career.

After opening the scoring in the 59th minute, Baartz was savagely chopped on the side of the neck by Uruguay's unscrupulous defender Luis Garisto, a hatchet man if ever there was one.

Baartz fell in a heap and was quickly taken off—never to play again—and was replaced by Alston.

"We learned afterwards about the severity of the injury," Alston recalled. "At first we thought he had just gone off injured … it happened all the time. But that night he got very ill and they quickly called Dr Brian Corrigan who got everything sorted and saved his life. The issue was one of the blood vessels that goes to the brain.

"Ray was subsequently told he could never play again, so his World Cup was over before it even started. It was very much an awkward time for the whole squad and the incident marred what should have been a memorable moment after beating two-time world champions Uruguay."

The Socceroos were beginning to understand why the world game was not always the 'beautiful game'.

Welcome to top class international football, Australia.

Chapter 8
Socceroos savour trip of a lifetime

In the days leading up to the start of the 1974 World Cup in West Germany, the Socceroos' players were fully focused on applying the finishing touches to their preparations for the stiffest challenge of their careers.

The trial matches were over, training sessions were less intense and for a long week it came down to being in the best frame of mind for the testing times ahead.

The intrepid Australians were due to meet both East Germany and West Germany in Hamburg, and Chile in Berlin in a very demanding Group 1. Coach Rasic was working overtime to get his part-time heroes ready for the big occasion.

The Australians were based at Bundesliga club SV Hamburg's plush complex outside the city and trained there twice a day.

At the end of each training session, all the 22 players in the squad were a picture of confidence and exuberance as the Australian and foreign media's attention on the part-time Socceroos intensified with the East Germany clash drawing closer and closer.

Alston, the long-haired, flamboyant striker they called 'Noddy' for his heading ability, was no different.

He was arguably the Socceroos' player with the highest profile and he exuded positivity and assurance whenever he was asked to talk about the impending challenge.

But behind his cocky exterior and happy-go-lucky persona, Alston had one major doubt in his mind.

It kept nagging him ever since the Australians had qualified for the World Cup finals thanks to that epic 1–0 victory over South Korea in Hong Kong in November.

You see, for all his goalscoring exploits and high stature—particularly since the Socceroos had kicked off their qualifying campaign 18 months earlier—Alston was not sure he would be Australia's main striker in the tournament in West Germany.

Coach Rasic was fully aware that the entire squad needed to be kept on its toes because complacency, over-confidence and a less-than-perfect preparation could jeopardise the campaign.

That is probably why he did not pick the same starting line-up in the nine matches leading up to the tournament, starting from the home fixtures against Ferencvaros and Uruguay early in the year.

The Australians then beat Indonesia in Jakarta and lost to Israel in Jaffa on their way to Europe, and in the fortnight prior to the start of the tournament they defeated Swiss clubs St Gallen, Young Boys and Neuchatel in three more trials.

Only fullback Utjesenovic, centre-half and captain Wilson and midfielder Jimmy Rooney started in each of the nine matches prior to the World Cup.

"I was confident of playing in the World Cup because I had been virtually a regular starter for the last 18 months or so but there was always a doubt at the back of your head because Rasic used to do things like changing our style of play according to the opposition's strengths and weaknesses," Alston explained.

"Sometimes we played with three strikers and on other occasions it was just one or two, so the trial matches gave us no idea as to how we would play in the World Cup.

"I'm sure Rasic had made his mind up on our formation and approach because he would have known everything there was to know about the opposition … but he wasn't letting on.

"He did his homework on all opponents we faced thanks to his contacts abroad and was not the type of coach to 'play the game and learn about the opposition as we go along'.

"He had a plan for everything and everyone and he wanted to keep us fully committed to the cause all the time by never giving us any clear indication as to who might be starting in the World Cup.

"He hardly ever picked the same 11 in the trials leading up to the tournament, starting with the two matches against Ferencvaros.

"There were several players vying for a starting spot, including Gary Manuel, Ernie Campbell and Peter Ollerton, who scored one of the goals against Uruguay in that infamous international a few weeks earlier.

"You know, it was just extraordinary that Ollerton came from Preston just like me. So while England failed to qualify for the World Cup after losing out to Poland, two boys from this little town in the north were able to go to the big dance."

Alston chose the trial match against St Gallen to make a case for a starting spot in the finals by scoring a quick-fire hat-trick that gave the Socceroos an impressive 4–1 victory.

"It was three goals in 11 minutes in the second half," he recalled. "I was sure that the hat-trick helped my case for selection."

Rasic left nothing to chance in his manic mission to give his players the best opportunity to give a solid account of themselves.

And he was understandably worried that the attention his players were getting from foreign scouts, agents and the media might disrupt the team's preparations.

He realised that none of his part-time players had experienced anything like that. Being only human, of course, it was very easy to be distracted. But Alston was adamant that this was never going to be a problem because all the players realised they had come too far and worked too hard to blow it by losing concentration.

"We had a job to do and there was no way anybody was going to get carried away and forget what we were there for," he insisted.

"We were a strong and united group of mates that looked out for each other and I've said this many times … I owe my success as a footballer to all my teammates but the Socceroos' sides of 1973 and 1974 were the best, the epitome.

"From the day we flew into Germany we were always busy, training twice a day, having fun at five-a-side, doing silly things and so on. I was one of the stupid ones. I used to try to sing but I came across as a bit of a comedian, which was just me. We had many laughs and thoroughly enjoyed every minute of each day in Hamburg and later in Berlin.

"The coach kept telling us, 'Make sure you have enough rest', but we were always on the go. We were never going to get bored, that's for sure."

The whole group was also fascinated by the high level of security that had been afforded to them throughout their stay in Germany.

The 1974 World Cup took place two years after the Black September terrorist attack that marred the Munich Olympics and the German organisers were understandably nervous.

Wherever they went in their big coach that had 'Australia' emblazoned in big letters on its sides, the Socceroos were escorted not by police but by armed soldiers. Guard dogs were ever present in the Hamburg complex.

The players were effectively living in isolation and no one was allowed to go out of the centre on his own.

The only time they got to enjoy the company of people from the outside world was when they had visits from family and when they talked to the media after training. The Australian players in the squad who were born in England were a prime target for the English media.

England had failed to qualify for the World Cup after coming a cropper against the Poles, and the stories about a bunch of part-timers who had defied the odds and made it to Germany while the high-profile millionaires in the English league had failed to qualify became very tasty, particularly for the tabloids.

"The English media was there all the time and at that St Gallen game too. England had failed to qualify so they were interested in me and the other 'English' players in the squad like Wilson, Ollerton and Ray Richards.

"The German media was also fascinated by the story behind 'milkman by night' Schaefer, for obvious reasons.

"The 'Scottish' like Rooney and Mackay got some attention too but it was rather limited because Scotland, unlike England, were in the tournament too.

"The media was making a beeline towards all of us, really, especially those of us who were naturalised Australians. And they certainly gave me the idea that I was being looked at by some clubs. You could tell with the way they were interviewing me.

"But we were always sheltered by Rasic. He allowed us to speak to the media for only a limited time after we finished training, then it was back on the bus to return to our camp.

"He was very strict with us. He probably did all this because he knew we were not used to this level of attention and scrutiny and he wanted us to keep our feet on the ground and concentrate solely on the job ahead of us."

After the traumatic incident in the Uruguay match that would spell an abrupt end for Baartz's career, Rasic wished to reward the unfortunate striker with a trip to Germany as a non-playing member of the delegation.

Firstly, Rasic wanted to show his appreciation for what Baartz had done for Australian football in general and the Socceroos in particular, and secondly, the coach was keen for the striker to be in Germany to lend his moral support to the 22 men in green and gold.

The whole playing group fully supported Rasic's gesture but, surprise, surprise, the Australian Soccer Federation refused to pay for Baartz's trip, fearing it would set a precedent if other players got injured in similar circumstances.

"I told the suits, 'Baartz is not any other player. You cannot treat the guy like a nobody'," Rasic said. "I got my way and Baartz came with us to Germany."

It was a costly victory, however, as post-World Cup events would prove.

Alston said Baartz's presence gave the whole squad a massive lift. "Every single one of us loved his football and of course we were delighted to find out that he was going to be with us. It was fantastic to see him there. It was very touching.

"It must have been very hard for him. I could not imagine being in his position and thinking 'I'm missing all this'."

As the day of the big kickoff approached, Alston was in his room with his regular roommate Abonyi when he received an unexpected telephone call.

"Our team interpreter Peter came to find me to tell me I had a phone call," Noddy recalled.

"The Hamburg complex was huge and I went down to the office to take the call and, would you believe it, my dad was on the line. He said, 'I'm here'. I replied, 'What do you mean you're here?' He said, 'I'm at the airport with Mum'.

"I said, 'Bloody hell, how did you two get here'? He explained that my wife Doreen (who was back home in Australia) had sent my parents two air tickets from England to Germany so they could watch me play in the World Cup.

"My dad then asked me if I could pick them up from the airport but I said, 'No way, I'm in camp'.

"My parents did not even have any accommodation organised but after I spoke to reporter David Jack of Sydney's *The Sun,* he kindly offered to give them his hotel room in town and he moved in with another journalist.

"The interpreter was happy to pick them up from the airport and I snuck out of camp to meet my parents.

"We players got two tickets each per game but, being rather resourceful, I managed to secure about 20 tickets from all those players who did not have family in Germany and had no one to give them to. I gave all the tickets to my dad who in turn forwarded some to the interpreter who was very helpful throughout our stay in Hamburg."

The Socceroos could not wait for the moment they stepped into the world spotlight for the opportunity to show that they were more than 'no-hopers and greenhorns'. That's how Berlin's mass circulation newspaper *Bild-Zeitung* described the Australian team. They subsequently issued a public apology at the end of the group phase.

The question was even asked in the German media why 'a bunch of kangaroos' were allowed to take part in such a big tournament.

However, most of Australia was behind the dedicated part-timers who dared to dream. The players were relishing a situation where, for once, they were given the acclaim and respect at home that they so richly deserved.

But with the accolades came the responsibility.

The players knew ever since that memorable night in Hong Kong that they had a golden opportunity to boost the game's image in Australia.

Football was seen as a poor relation to other big winter sports like Australian rules and rugby league.

But the growing interest shown by the media in the Socceroos' achievement of reaching their first World Cup—which comprised only 16 teams in those days—had given the players a degree of responsibility to do well not just for their colours and their careers, but for the game in general.

They were sporting missionaries.

"The two coaches, Rasic and (assistant) Les Scheinflug, made it quite clear from the very beginning what we were all about and what we could achieve for the game in our country with a positive performance," Alston said.

"But sadly, after we came back from Germany, the soccer federation let it go by. They could have done so much more with the Socceroos' 'brand'. They could have changed the face of football in Australia but all they did was say, 'It's all over now and it's back to normal, that's it'."

Now where have we heard that one?

Chapter 9
Alston the centre of attention

It was the most bruising match of his career but it did not bother ambitious Alston one bit. He regarded the torrid tussle with one of Europe's hardest defenders as the price he had to pay to realise his dream of playing in the World Cup.

On 15 June 1974, the Socceroos' striker was chosen to lead the line in Australia's baptism of fire against East Germany in Hamburg.

It certainly was a red-letter day in his career that was going places.

East German football was seen as the new force of the European game in the mid-1970s even though its fall would be as quick and dramatic as its rise from relative obscurity.

The national team had seen off Romania to qualify for its first ever World Cup and Magdeburg FC, with Jurgen Sparwasser leading their attack, were fresh from beating AC Milan 2–0 in the UEFA Cup Winners' Cup final for the country's first major club honour only a few weeks earlier.

The Australian underdogs gave a good account of themselves in the rarefied air of the World Cup. They held out for almost an hour before conceding two goals that gave the Germans a 2–0 victory in Group 1 at the Volksparkstadion in Hamburg.

Hosts West Germany and Chile were the other teams in the group.

Alston was forced by tactical necessity to play a lone striker's role and had to deal with Konrad Weiss, one of Europe's toughest man markers who played his club football for Carl Zeiss Jena.

Alston's battle with Weiss was one of the highlights of the evening and the defender used every trick in the book to stop the tall Australian who was on top of his game.

Twice in the first half Alston made a mockery of the stopper's reputation. The defender was bamboozled by his footwork and conceded fouls that would have earned him at least a yellow card in today's environment.

"That guy was obviously given the task of marking me and he did the job on me alright because he kicked me all night," Alston recalled.

"I managed to beat him with the ball a few times in a one-on-one situation but every time I got away from him, he fouled me and he never even got a card.

"If that was today he would have had two yellows for persistent fouling and got sent off for sure.

"It was very hard in them days to hold the ball up and be constantly kicked up your arse while you're waiting for support. It was a bloody difficult job."

However, after each infringement, Alston got up, dusted himself off and proceeded to provide his team with an outlet up front to relieve the considerable pressure that their fitter and stronger opponents were applying.

Class always wins in the end, they say, and a few minutes before halftime with the Australians enjoying a spell of possession in the opposition's half, Alston chose to make a magnificent manoeuvre that he had done several times in Australia to humble Weiss.

The Australian got on to a long clearance from goalkeeper Jack Reilly and was pushed away from the penalty area towards the left wing by Weiss. There he beat the defender with an exquisite turn that would be immortalised by the great Johan Cruyff five days later when the Netherlands drew with Sweden in a Group 3 match.

Alston was facing his own goal and put his body between the ball and Weiss. He feigned a pass backwards and instead dragged the ball behind him with the inside of his right boot, pivoted 180 degrees on his standing left foot and he was gone, leaving the defender for dead.

"I had done it before at training and in league games but obviously I was never on television or playing at such a high-profile event as the World Cup, and when the opportunity in Hamburg arose, I just did it again. It was impulsive," he explained.

"Weiss was beaten all ends up and I was away, but my joy was short-lived because he chopped me at my legs. Again, he did not even get a card.

"Cruyff did the same move a few days later and it became known as the 'Cruyff turn', but hey, I did it first … at that level anyway."

Alston's turn was probably the moment that epitomised his impressive performance. It raised a few eyebrows among the onlookers and television viewers who would have known very little about any of the members of the team in green and gold.

Agents would also have been intrigued by this tall striker who gave East Germany's tough guys at the back a few headaches. At 26, Alston was at his peak.

"I was quite happy with my performance but I also was filthy I did not do more by scoring a goal," he said. "You're always striving for something else, I suppose.

"Unfortunately, it was impossible to speak to my parents after the game but I'm sure they would have been proud of the way I played."

The World Cup fever that had gripped the squad since it arrived in West Germany went up a few degrees after Rasic announced the line-up for the first match.

The formation did not contain any major surprises. It consisted of Reilly in goal; a back four of Utjesenovic, Wilson, Schaefer and Curran; a five-man midfield featuring

Warren, Mackay, Richards, Rooney and Buljevic, and Alston up front.

"I'm sure it was the day before the match that Rasic gave us the news after training," Alston recalled.

"It's funny, when you're a player it is easy to get your blinkers on and wonder if you're going to play rather than look at who's in the team.

"You tend to focus on yourself and I was a bit concerned a few days earlier because I had a rash on my face and Rasic left me out of a training session. I must have eaten too many strawberries in Switzerland on our way to Germany.

"I got the nod to start in the end. It was obvious from the line-up and the coach's team talk that we were going to play it prudently against the Germans and I was to be the one up front, wearing my No. 12.

"I didn't particularly like that number at first but then I looked at Gerd Muller who had a No. 13 jersey and Cruyff who was No. 14 … not a bad forward trio, eh?"

The whole squad went for a light run and had their stretches on the morning of the match and hung around at their accommodation complex after lunch, getting ready for the big match in the evening.

Alston and the rest of the starting players were raring to go but ever since Rasic had announced his line-up, the striker had the awkward job of trying to console his roommate and good friend Abonyi who had missed out on selection. His spot was taken by Warren.

"Atti was absolutely devastated," Alston recalled.

"He was a super-confident player and a great goalscorer and he proved this throughout his career. He must have been convinced he would play.

"It was tough to take for him and when you're playing in the biggest game of your life and your roommate is not in the team, what do you say to the guy? It was really hard. We were close and we still are like brothers.

"The thing about his non-selection was tactical. In away games—or in the ones that were very difficult as was the DDR [East Germany] match—Rasic tended to play with one striker and since Atti was a classic No. 10 and not a midfielder, it went against him in this instance.

"Rasic wanted to stack our midfield and he must have thought Buljevic and Warren were better suited for that job. We had to be cautious because we could have been beaten heavily had we opted for a more adventurous approach.

"I think the coach did the right thing, I've got to say. It's easy for me to say, 'Oh yeah put Atti alongside me', but who would have filled up the gap created in midfield?

"Warren had come back from his ACL and had worked himself back in the reckoning for selection."

The crowd at the Volksparkstadion was not huge. There were a few Australians and East Germans but the bulk of the attendance comprised German fans who made it clear they were there to support the Socceroos for two reasons.

Firstly, because everybody in sport has a soft spot for an underdog, and secondly, the West German fans were hoping the Socceroos would spring a surprise and take a point or two from their team's main rivals in the section.

Towards the end of the first half when the Socceroos mounted a few attacks, chants of 'Australien, Australien' rained from the terraces.

Earlier, just before the national anthems were played, a brief hush descended on the ground and Alston was blown away to hear his dad yelling at him from the main stand.

"He was offering his encouragement, yelling 'They're only 11, they're only 11'," he said. "That scenario could so easily have unfolded during a youth game in some little ground in the north of England, but here we were at the World Cup at the ground of Bundesliga big shots, SV Hamburg."

Formalities over, it came down to business. Alston had Buljevic to his left and Warren to his right in the centre-circle, and with his left foot he kicked off Australia's maiden World Cup campaign. History was made.

The Australians tried their best to crowd their midfield to stifle the Germans' expected initiative and stop them from arriving at Reilly's 'fort' in big numbers.

And when the Socceroos got the ball, they invariably tried to find Alston with long balls from defence over the top of the Germans' midfield.

Their tactics worked beautifully for a long time because the Socceroos limited the Germans to only two half-hearted efforts on goal in the first hour before star striker Sparwasser for once got away from his marker. He slid the ball past Reilly before Curran hit the ball into his own net in his valiant attempt to clear.

East Germany added another goal thanks to a superb shot from Joachim Streich to seal a vital win that would help them win the group ahead of their 'cousins' from the west.

"At first, we were all shattered with the result because we had worked hard and had played a good match against a world-class team," Alston explained.

"But Rasic told us he was not too disheartened by the result because he had seen a brave effort from us. He picked us up and let us know he was more than happy with the way we played and did everything that he expected of us.

"He insisted if the first own goal had not gone in, anything could have happened because the Germans were beginning to get very nervous about their inability to break us down. Frustration was beginning to creep into their game.

"So we just took the defeat on the chin and started thinking about the next game. That's the way we were."

Despite the initial defeat, Alston had seen enough of the World Cup to regard just being there as the undisputed highlight of his career.

The magnitude of the event, the surreal atmosphere surrounding it, the quality of football on show, the treatment of players, the huge media presence and what the game meant to the fans in a proper soccer country blew Alston and his teammates away.

It was like they were playing on another planet.

"Playing in England was always my goal, which I would reach after the tournament," he said. "But the World Cup was 10 times better.

"It was unbelievable and after the first match, I remember saying to myself, 'I can have more of this'.

"It's massive, no doubt the pinnacle of any footballer's ambition. It's bigger than the Olympics."

The World Cup adventure was not going to get any easier. Next up was European champions, West Germany.

Chapter 10
In the court of football royalty

Coach Rasic had a special job for his lone striker Alston in Australia's group match against hosts West Germany in the 1974 World Cup.

The Socceroos had lost their first match in the tournament to East Germany by two goals to nil.

However, they had played reasonably well and managed to hold out their stronger opponents for an hour before conceding two goals, one of them being an own goal.

But European champions West Germany were a different proposition and would prove to be an even harder nut to crack.

West German football was enjoying great success at both international and club level in the mid-'70s.

The national team under Helmut Schoen's leadership had won the 1972 European Championship in Belgium amid widespread recognition and was chasing a rare double in the World Cup on home soil.

And Bundesliga giants Bayern Munich had just snared the first of three straight European Cups after crushing Atletico Madrid 4-0 in a replayed final only a few weeks earlier.

It was a measure of the kind of challenge the part-time Socceroos were facing that six of the players that helped Bayern win the continental title were in the starting line-up when the two teams met at the Volksparkstadion in Hamburg in front of 53,000 spectators who were expecting a goal fest.

The six Bayern players were goalkeeper Sepp Maier, sweeper Franz Beckenbauer, stopper Hans-Jorg Schwarzenbeck, fullback Paul Breitner, midfielder Uli Hoeness and striker Gerd Muller.

The side was so strong that there was no place anymore for Borussia Monchengladbach hero Gunther Netzer, who starred in Germany's Euro '72 triumph.

Rasic was fully aware of the influence Beckenbauer exerted on the whole side and recognised the mayhem 'Kaiser Franz' could cause when he left his sweeper's role to orchestrate his team's movements with his majestic and nonchalant stride.

This is where Noddy came in.

Football can throw up all sorts of unexpected and illogical confrontations, but the scenario involving a Safeway United striker from the little suburb of Woonona having to deal with a Bayern superstar from a high-profile city like Munich at the highest level of the game would have been hard to imagine, let alone beat.

"Apart from my job up front which was never going to be easy, Rale gave me specific instructions to keep an eye on Beckenbauer when the Germans had the ball and try to stop him from running the show all day from midfield," he explained.

"I tried to do that but sometimes I was 30 metres away from him and by the time I got there, he had taken off. I did that a couple of times and what he did after that was wander up to midfield because he knew I would follow him. The problem was that in doing so he took me out of the attack and we had no one up front. Smart guy."

Rasic was not expected to tinker with the line-up or formation of the team in arguably the most daunting challenge the Australians had ever faced.

The pragmatic coach made one change from the side that fell honourably to East Germany. Warren picked up a foot injury in that first match and was ruled out. He was replaced by fellow striker Ernie Campbell in a nominal 4-3-3 formation.

But once again the Socceroos realistically would play with five in the middle because strikers Campbell and Buljevic were instructed to drop back.

The line-up was: Reilly; Utjesenovic, Wilson, Schaefer, Curran; Mackay, Richards, Rooney; Campbell, Alston, Buljevic.

If the Australians managed to cope quite well with the East Germans for the best part of the match, they soon discovered that the West Germans were a far more skilful and merciless side.

At the start of matchday two, East Germany had a goal difference of plus two after their win over the Socceroos, while Germany was plus one after beating Chile 1-0.

Goals and points were therefore important because they could determine the top positions in the group.

Captain Beckenbauer as usual was directing all the traffic from the back in his inimitable manner, but the flow was one-way. The slick Germans, with the crowd firmly behind them, dominated the first half and led at the break with goals from Cologne pair Wolfgang Overath and Bernd Cullmann, and it could have been worse.

Muller hit the bar with a glorious diving header and Hoeness steered the ball wide from a favourable position before Reilly did very well to stop a fierce, rising shot from Berti Vogts.

In the second half, Muller made it three with a glancing header from a corner but Germany failed to add to their tally.

Alston, who was described by Schoen as the Socceroos' most dangerous player after watching the striker's performance in the first match, was clearly a marked man and would be the only one to trouble the Germans.

Schoen would have reckoned that if Alston were kept quiet, then the Socceroos could never hurt his team so he gave hard man Schwarzenbeck the task of shadowing the Australian for most of the match.

It was a terrific tussle between the two. On one occasion in the first half, Alston justified Schoen's concerns when he played a wall pass with Campbell, dribbled past Schwarzenbeck, sped towards goal and moved away from Beckenbauer before having a shot that missed the target.

Alston was clearly enjoying himself in the court of football royalty and in the second half he created a genuine chance to open his and Australia's scoring account.

He picked up the ball in midfield and again flew past Schwarzenbeck with consummate ease. Before Beckenbauer, as the last man, could put in a challenge, he hit a fierce, low drive that Maier saved.

Alston knew straight away that he should have done better.

"I rushed my shot a little bit because I was worried about Beckenbauer who was coming in to tackle me," he said.

"In a game like that when you get only a few opportunities to shoot on goal, you should make the most of any scoring chance.

"It was my fault, actually. I should have steadied myself a bit more—perhaps taken another touch—and try to place the ball in the far corner rather than hit it hard straight at Maier."

Towards the end of the match, Alston had to leave the field for a few minutes after suffering from cramps. It was the only time in the contest that he did not feel Schwarzenbeck breathing down his neck.

"I was as fit as anybody else but playing up front and coming into action only occasionally and having to jump for headers to meet long balls from defence will test your muscles," he said.

"The team doctor wanted to give me an injection but I told him not to worry about it. I was playing okay and I could not wait to go back on the field and finish the game, which I did. I was not going to miss any more time on the sidelines in the biggest game of my life. I would have played on even with one leg."

The Australians, despite being outplayed, never stopped trying and a few minutes from the end Abonyi, who had come on for Campbell at the start of the second half, was desperately unlucky not to put Australia on the scoresheet when his well-placed shot hit the post with Maier beaten.

The Socceroos were thus eliminated from the World Cup after two defeats.

They gave a very good account of themselves against the East Germans but the West Germans were something else. Too strong, too skilful and too clever, basically.

The Socceroos' brave performances received widespread acclaim but those in

Australia who did not fully appreciate the high quality of the opposition might have been disappointed with Australia's reluctance to have a go in the two matches.

Alston was adamant it would have been suicidal to face such excellent opponents openly, and besides, he claimed that sometimes it is the sheer class of the opposition that forces you to defend and there is nothing you can do about it.

"Ok, many said we played defensively in both matches but sometimes you just cannot control those things, especially when you are playing against a much better team," he protested.

"You have to defend because they are that good going forward, especially the West Germans. Even West Germany's fullbacks Vogts and Breitner were relentless. They were non-stop.

"Every single player in that team was unbelievably talented. In every match that you play for your country, you must expect top opposition and no weak links because you are facing the chosen few. But in West Germany's case, they had a superstar in every position.

"You just stood there and took in the fact that you were playing the world's biggest team in the world's biggest competition with the whole world watching and you were part of it. It was an awesome feeling.

"Looking back, the shot from Overath that found the net after only 12 minutes probably came too early because we did not have too much time to get into the groove. That goal put a spanner in the works. The first goal in any match is very important because it forces the team that concedes to come out and concede more space to the opposition.

"But if the truth be told, the Germans were awesome and they proved their worth by beating an excellent Dutch side in the final to win the World Cup.

"And you know what? Those days the World Cup was a 16-team competition so spots in the finals were at a premium. We had to win all the time at every stage of the qualifying campaign or else we were gone. There was never a second chance like there is today."

The match ended somewhat controversially when the Hamburg crowd gave the German team the bird for not scoring more goals. They thought the home team had taken its foot off the pedal after scoring the third goal, but the reality was that the proud Australians fought bravely not to be embarrassed.

"Of course we were determined. We respected them, but we were never going to let them humiliate us. That's just not us," Alston explained.

"The crowd was getting agitated towards the end because the spectators were probably expecting more goals, but we did not let them do that."

Beckenbauer, who as a Bayern legend from the south was not as popular a figure in northern Hamburg, bore the brunt of the jeering and at one stage he reacted angrily to the boos.

"Beckenbauer said after the game that the team was surprised with our determination," he said.

"I would like to think that our overall performance had changed a few people's minds about our football, especially those who questioned our right to be in the competition in the first place."

There was no doubt in Alston's mind that he had the greatest experience of his football life on that remarkable afternoon at the Volksparkstadion. And what made it an even more memorable affair was the fact that he managed to secure Beckenbauer's green No. 5 jersey.

The legendary defender was still rather annoyed with the crowd's behaviour when the match was over, yet he honoured a promise he would give Alston his jersey despite Wilson's attempt to snare the shirt for himself.

Alston needed a degree of smartness and anticipation that he often found handy in opposing penalty boxes to secure such a prized bit of football memorabilia. He would give it to his son Adrian later when he was old enough to appreciate it.

"We arrived at the ground one and a half hours from kickoff and to our surprise we found out that the Germans were already warming up," Alston recalled.

"We said to ourselves that by the time the match started, they would be knackered.

"The group went into our dressing room to prepare but I did not follow the lads to the sheds and instead I went over to where Beckenbauer was warming up, and when he was done I got in early and asked him if we could exchange jerseys after the match.

"He asked me what number I would be wearing and when I said my jersey number was 12 he said, 'Ok, I'll look out for you'.

"I said to him, 'Don't you worry about that, mate, I'll be looking out for you wherever you are.'"

Noddy would do that in more ways than one that day.

Chapter 11
Rasic unleashes his 'three gangsters'

After losing the opening two matches of the 1974 World Cup, the Socceroos left their home away from home in Hamburg and travelled to Berlin to face Chile in what many Australian fans regarded as a bit of an anti-climax.

Rasic's men had been eliminated but not embarrassed after two losses against mighty East Germany and mightier West Germany.

Yet the pride and spirit that were the hallmark of an indomitable bunch of players ensured there was no way the Socceroos would treat the fixture as a dead rubber.

"We were determined not to come away from the tournament without a point and losing again did not even enter our minds, such was our desire to get something out of the Chile game," Alston remembered.

"We knew the Chileans would provide us with a stiff challenge because they were highly ranked, but that also gave us another motive to do well against them.

"We never even considered the fixture as a dead rubber. That is not the way we were. We went out there to have a go at Chile and you could see that by the line-up that Rasic picked. For the first time in the tournament, we had Abonyi, me and Buljevic starting up front with clear instructions to be more attack-minded than in the previous two matches.

"We desperately wanted to win that game, no doubt about that, and we were hugely disappointed that we did not beat them and had to settle for a 0–0 draw.

"It was pleasing to get a point of course but, to be honest, we wanted the two points badly, so in a way we saw the 'positive' result as a 'negative'.

"Not scoring one goal in the whole tournament was also deflating from the team's perspective. We had decent chances against West Germany.

"On a personal level, it would have been nice to get a goal and have my name etched in the game's history books, especially since I thought I had a good World Cup. It would have been nice to put the icing on the cake by putting one in, but that's life and there is not much you can do about that."

Rasic could have given some fringe players an opportunity to play, but he was taking no chances because he wanted Australia to sign off with victory over the South Americans.

He kept faith with the same team that started the second half against West Germany. It meant that Abonyi, who performed very strongly after coming on for Campbell and who was unlucky to hit the post with a well-placed shot, retained his place to get his first start.

The team was Reilly; Utjesenovic, Wilson, Schaefer, Curran; Mackay, Richards, Rooney; Abonyi, Alston, Buljevic.

The formation featured a front trio of serial thrillers that Rasic called 'the three gangsters' and looked hungry and more adventurous, but the Chileans, who needed a win at all costs to stay in the tournament, were soon on the front foot.

There were no simultaneous group fixtures on matchday three in those days. The clash in Berlin kicked off three and a half hours before the German 'derby' in Hamburg.

Chile sought to beat the Socceroos by more than one goal and hoped West Germany could do the job on their 'cousins' from the east.

The Socceroos' valiant attempt to not go home scoreless and pointless was evident from the first minutes. They fought for every ball as if their lives depended on it— defending vigorously whenever they were under pressure and attacking without hesitation when given the chance.

On one occasion in the second half, Mackay blazed over the bar from two metres out after being served by the overlapping Curran.

The match was marred by a massive downpour during halftime and the break lasted more than 20 minutes. But a waterlogged pitch that made it hard for players to control the ball, let alone keep their balance, did not deter Rasic's men. They even survived a red card for Richards to snare a point.

Richards received the second of two yellow cards late in the match but continued to play. Iranian referee Jafar Ramdar had forgotten all about the first infringement in the first half. However, he was alerted to his mistake by the linesman five minutes later and amid the ensuing confusion, he gave the midfielder another yellow and a red.

Richards thus became the first player to be given three yellow cards and a red card in one single World Cup match!

Defender Harry Williams also made history by becoming the first Indigenous player to play in the World Cup when he came on for Curran eight minutes from time. This substitution came after Alston was replaced by Ollerton in the 66th minute. His World Cup odyssey was over.

Not conceding a goal was not something to sneer at, of course. Forty-eight years and 16 finals matches later, the Socceroos are still searching for another World Cup clean sheet.

East Germany surprisingly beat West Germany 1–0 later in the day to win the group.

At the end of the campaign that provided him with three matches he would never forget, Alston was able to sit back, put his feet up and take in the enormity of his and his teammates' achievement of reaching the finals.

He had met the challenge of facing some of the world's finest teams and toughest defenders head-on. The kid from Ribbleton in suburban Preston came away with an uplifting feeling that he belonged at the highest level of the game.

The long journey that started with an away qualifying match against New Zealand at the modest Newmarket Ground in Auckland in early 1973 ended with a match against Chile at Berlin's Olympiastadion, one of the world's most famous sporting grounds.

Berlin's impressive stadium was the main venue of the 1936 Olympics, and it later hosted the 2006 World Cup final.

"Looking back at the whole experience, my personal highlight was playing future world champions West Germany in a packed stadium in Hamburg and swapping shirts with Beckenbauer after the match," Alston reminisced with pride.

"Walking out for our first game against East Germany and listening to our 'Advance Australia Fair' anthem gave us all an unbelievable thrill, too, but the West Germany occasion was something else. I had come from this little town in England's north and I was rubbing shoulders with the game's elite. It was just wonderful and I will never ever forget those two magical weeks. We got paid very little for our efforts, but to be honest, I would have done it for nothing and would do it all over again for nothing. That's how much the whole World Cup experience meant to me.

"Personally, I was always well supported by the coaches, my teammates and [the] whole staff. I cannot stress strongly enough my gratitude for the backing I got in Germany."

The Socceroos' overall record in the tournament was met with scepticism in some quarters, particularly from those who either did not fully appreciate the enormity of the challenge the semi-professional players had faced, or those who grasped an opportunity to have a go at a game that was still seen as foreign by elements within the mainstream media.

Many observers thought that the team should have been less pragmatic and more adventurous in its general approach, but Alston wouldn't have a bar of this.

"In hindsight, everybody would have a story. Logically, you just cannot say we should have done this or done that," Alston claimed.

"That's just easy pickings to start pointing the finger at somebody. And it's totally unnecessary.

"There was not much we could do against the two German sides but we went after the Chileans, so it was not always backs-to-the-wall stuff. Rasic is no fool and he knew that we could not possibly play openly in the first two games because we would have thrown ourselves to the wind.

"But he would have thought that beating Chile was a distinct possibility and the fact that he picked Abonyi—who is an attacking player—proved that.

"The bottom line is we did the best we could under the circumstances presented to us. All in all, we did well and it was satisfying to see so many fans welcoming us back home after we touched down in Sydney.

"Most people had expected us to get smashed and I'd like to think that many of them were surprised by our results that were not too bad despite the fact we had failed to score.

"German coaches, players and media people were certainly surprised by our football, not least the newspaper that had described us as no-hopers. It graciously offered us an apology after our three matches. There were many others who should have said sorry to us, too."

The squad had a couple of days off in Berlin after the Chile match before they made the long trek home. Most players took the opportunity to relax, see some of the sights, take in a few bars and do some shopping.

Some also spent time with their families that had made the trip to Germany, while Alston's regular roommate Abonyi went to Hungary to see some of his relatives.

"My parents, who were absolutely delighted with Australia's fighting spirit and proud of my performance, had gone home after our second match, and since Atti went to Hungary to see some of his folks, I was left in my room on my own and did a bit of this and that. I also had time to consider my club future," he said. (More on that in the next chapter).

Alston, who was still a Safeway United player, and the rest of the squad were in high spirits when they returned to Australia. They were happy to see their families and friends but they soon got the shock of their lives.

Soon after touching down in Sydney they learned that Rasic, the man who had changed their lives and helped make their dreams come true, was sacked by the Australian Soccer Federation.

Rasic did not return home with the squad because he honoured a promise to work with the German media when Australia's involvement in the event ended. He would have known that the end of his tenure was near due to his many disagreements with the federation, but he never let on because he kept his kerfuffles with officialdom to himself.

"We had done a wonderful job and we were over the moon," Alston said. "We honestly believed that the game would take off straight away and go berserk. We also hoped that the state leagues would become more professional where players did not have to do other jobs.

"But it wasn't to be. Football had shot itself in the foot once again. We could not believe what we were hearing about Rasic. It was like snapping the head off our game.

"The drama with Rasic should never have happened. He would have added to that squad and made it better. Some players had expressed their desire to quit international football after the World Cup, but there were other young players coming through and already some of us were thinking of the qualifiers for 1978.

"Clearly Rale was sacked because he was never prepared to be a yes man. It was always an issue with him ... he always put his players first and it had to be his way and some people from the federation did not like that."

Alston had sacrificed a lot to realise his dream of playing in the World Cup. All up, he had lost four jobs since making his debut for the national team against Greece in Sydney in 1969.

As a part-time footballer, it would have been a difficult decision to toss away a secure job when his family needed to be raised and his mortgage needed to be paid.

So how did he explain to his wife Doreen why he had quit his jobs to play football, effectively for peanuts?

"My family certainly sacrificed a lot," Alston explained. "I did too but it definitely was worth it. Football was my life.

"I loved the game and I would do it all over again, but I would be a lot smarter about it and look after myself better financially. I would plan my future better. I was always a 'what will be will be' sort of bloke. I lived for the day.

"Doreen never complained or questioned my decisions. She was always behind me and sacrificed a lot for me. So I was never in a difficult position. She had a sporting background too. She was a sprinter in Preston and used to take part in the Lancashire championships ... and had to give all that away to follow me in Australia. So she understood what football meant to me and why it was so important."

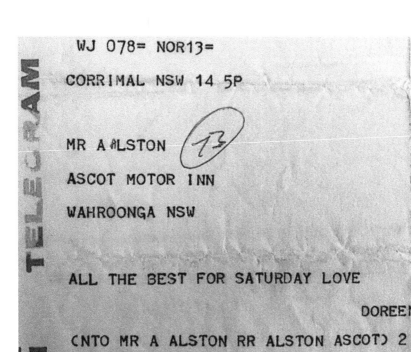

TELEGRAM

```
WJ 078= NOR13=

CORRIMAL NSW 14 5P

MR A ALSTON        13

ASCOT MOTOR INN

WAHROONGA NSW


ALL THE BEST FOR SATURDAY LOVE

                                    DOREEN

(NTO MR A ALSTON RR ALSTON ASCOT) 2
```

A telegram from Doreen prior to Alston's Socceroos debut in 1969.

Celebrating a St George Budapest grand final win with teammate Manfred Schaefer, 1970.

Alston signed with St George Budapest in 1970 after a season with South Coast United.

At an international friendly against Greece in Athens, November 1970. Australia won 3-1.

Playing for St George Budapest, 1971.

An Australian XI met Dundee in Adelaide, May 1972. Alston is facing the camera.

From L-R: Peter Wilson, Atti Abonyi and Alston celebrating the 3-0 win against Iran in a World Cup qualifier at the Sydney Sports Ground, August 1973.

In a warm-up match for the 1974 World Cup against Neuchatel FC in Switzerland. Ilano Mantoan for Neuchatel (L) battles Alston for the ball (R). Australia won 0-1.

With Socceroos teammates in Hamburg, West Germany, in 1974. From L-R: Col Curran, Ivo Rudic, Doug Utjesenovic, Alston, and Max Tolson.

Lining-up for the match in Hamburg against East Germany at the 1974 World Cup. East Germany won 2-0.

Challenged by Franz Beckenbauer in the match against West Germany at the 1974 World Cup, played in Hamburg. West Germany won 3-0.

With Doreen and young Adrian on our way to Luton Town, August 1974.

Alston's first day at Luton Town in 1974, signing an autograph for a young fan with Luton Town's manager Harry Haslam.

Playing for Luton Town against West Ham, October 1974. The match ended 0-0.

Scoring for Luton Town against Peter Shilton's Leicester, April 1975. Luton Town won the match 3-0.

Alston with Peter Stone at Sydney Airport returning from a friendly match against Singapore, November 1977. Australia won 0-2.

Celebrating a goal for Tampa Bay Rowdies, 1977.

Prior to a Tampa Bay Rowdies vs New York Cosmos match, 1977.
From L-R: Franz Beckenbauer (Cosmos), Alston, Pelé, Giorgio Chinaglia (both Cosmos), and Rowdies teammate Len Glover.

With boxing father, Alec.

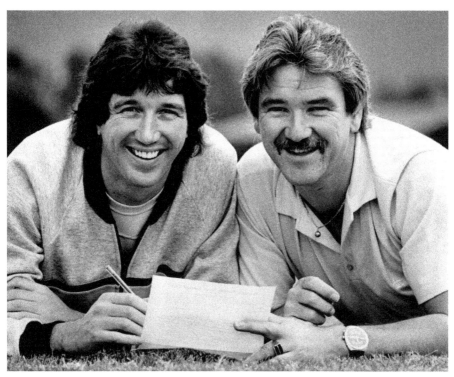

Signing to coach Corrimal Rangers with Terry Hurley, 1984.

Watching from the bench as coach of Corrimal Rangers, 1985.

Alston today with the jersey worn by Franz Beckenbauer in the World Cup match between Australia and West Germany in 1974.

Chapter 12
Alston snubs Bundesliga

The 1974 World Cup was the most amazing and uplifting experience of Alston's career. He would have been entitled to feel like he had seen it all as an international footballer, but a curious incident in the latter stages of Australia's match with Chile in Berlin blew him away.

The Socceroos were playing the South Americans in the third and final match of their group at the awe-inspiring Olympic Stadium.

The men in green and gold were already eliminated after two defeats but were seeking to sign off from the tournament with a morale-boosting victory over a strong opponent.

And with the score still goalless in the 66th minute, Rasic made a change in a bid to break the deadlock.

He wanted some fresh legs for a final fling at the Chileans in wet conditions. He brought on Ollerton for his main striker Alston who was showing signs of fatigue after battling bravely and endlessly throughout the campaign.

Alston went off, did not bother with a shower, changed into some dry clothes and rushed back onto the field to savour the last few moments of his World Cup adventure. He joined Rasic and the subs on the Australian bench.

Then he was taken aback by something that came completely out of the blue.

A gentleman claiming to be an official from Bundesliga giants Hertha Berlin approached him—while the match was still going on—and told him the club would like to sign him. He gave him a contract to sign.

Alston had experienced many extraordinary moments in his life—seeing Sydney Harbour for the first time was one of them—but this one topped the lot. It was like something you'd read in the comics.

"I already knew that Hertha and two other German clubs were interested in me, and of course I told them I was not going to do anything before the end of the World Cup," Alston said.

"Nobody could get near us in Germany—not even my parents—so all approaches were done over the phone, and as soon as I sat down on the bench, this bloke came up to me and over my shoulder he shoved a contract in front of me and encouraged me to sign it.

"I could not believe what I was seeing. He wanted me to sign there and then but how could I do that … apart from the fact that it was in German? I just had to say to him, 'Mate, let's finish this match first eh … then we can talk'. I felt embarrassed because the players on the bench saw what was going on and were jumping on me and urging me to sign up."

The Hertha representative did not give up. That same evening, during a reception for the team at a brewery, the club officially approached Alston and offered him a three-year contract with a signing-on fee of $40,000.

He had other unofficial offers from two more Bundesliga clubs (Hamburg and Eintracht Frankfurt) but Hertha was more serious and forthcoming in their approach. That's what made up Alston's mind.

It was an offer too good to refuse and one that would change both his and his young family's lives.

Alston was sold on the idea of being a full-time professional in one of the world's strongest and most respected leagues and being able to call the Olympiastadion his home ground. In no time, he and the club agreed on terms.

A transfer fee between Safeway and Hertha had yet to be arranged of course, but Alston knew all along that the club would not stand in his way. Safeway would not object to his move when Alston returned home and told club boss Birch about the offer, especially since the club would get something like $100,000 for letting him go.

This would be a particularly sound piece of business because Alston's return to Safeway from St George in 1972 had only cost the south coast club $5,000.

Noddy also knew that his wife Doreen, who had no idea what was going on behind the scenes in Germany, would have had no hesitation in following him in Germany.

When Alston arrived home and started a new season with Safeway, the two clubs verbally agreed on a substantial transfer fee and for all intents and purposes he and his family were preparing for a new life in one of the great cities of Europe.

In the meantime, English First Division club Luton, who had not forgotten Alston's strong performance in a Socceroos' world tour match way back in 1970 when he scored in a 2–1 win, must have been impressed by his admirable skill and commitment shown in the World Cup.

The Hatters, who had just been promoted to the top division, saw an opportunity to boost their limited ranks. They put the cat among the pigeons by going in strongly for the striker who was at the peak of his career.

"Don Shanks, who was a Luton player on loan to south coast club Balgownie at the time, came to see me and the next minute the club's secretary flew in with a three-year contract and signing-on fee that were similar to Hertha's. They also matched the Berlin club's bid," Alston explained.

"The new offer threw me, and in the end, I chose Luton. The prospect of returning to England and playing in the First Division just like my brother Alec did was too strong to knock back, especially since it also meant a lot to my family and Doreen's.

"Preston showed some interest, but nothing came of it.

"We had been away from England since 1968 and by joining Luton and living in the south in Bedfordshire, we would be able to phone our families up in Preston any time rather than rely on communicating by post. More importantly, our families would be only a four-hour drive away, not a 24-hour flight that would have cost us an arm and a leg.

"The language was a factor too, but looking back, I have to say that I should have gone to the Bundesliga. It was the biggest mistake I ever made. It was the only time I put family first and football second."

Even Beckenbauer himself would tell him later when they crossed paths in the North American Soccer League that he was "very surprised" he chose to snub Germany and go to a country that had not even made it to the World Cup.

The English football landscape at the top level was very different to what it is today when Alston, his wife and his son moved to Bedfordshire, north of London, at the start of season 1974–75.

Tommy Docherty's Manchester United were in Division Two after being relegated in the previous season and Derby County would win the championship.

Queens Park Rangers would finish the season as the highest-placed London team in 11th spot and Luton would be dragged into a relegation dogfight with Tottenham Hotspur and Chelsea.

"My stay at Kenilworth Road would become a lovely experience because, once again, everybody was wonderful to me and helped me adapt to my new surroundings," he said.

"To be honest, I felt that their pre-season training was not what I needed because I had been playing full-on for a long time and I was super fit and super sharp. Yet would you believe it, the coaches at the club told me I needed to get fitter, so for the first few weeks of the season it was just plodding around and doing 10-mile runs every day.

"I was not trying to be a smartarse but I told them I did not need that because I was ready to start the season, so all that physical training pulled me back by a couple of months because after a while I began to lose my sharpness.

"Having said that, I started the season quite well as long as the grounds were good. I remember getting the man-of-the-match award after scoring and hitting the post in a 2–2 draw with Arsenal at Highbury. I just loved the atmosphere at that match and it was probably the highlight of my time with Luton.

"I also remember jumping off the bus near the ground and I saw a newspaper poster saying, 'Aussie takes on the Gunners'. I was very proud of that.

"Things were looking up generally, but I went off the boil a bit before Christmas when the weather started to change and the pitches became heavier … we were running around in mud most of the time. I'm not making excuses because it was the same for everybody. I still managed about 22 matches and eight goals though, which was satisfying. I ended up as the club's joint top scorer with Ron Futcher.

"It would have been nice to play at Old Trafford, for example, but at that time Man United were just not good enough to be there."

In his first season in English football, Alston also fulfilled his childhood dream of playing in the fabled FA Cup, yet his participation was brief because Luton lost 1–0 to Birmingham in the third round.

The League Cup provided Alston with better rewards because he scored his first goal for Luton with a header in a 1–0 victory over Bristol Rovers, but they lost 2–0 to Sheffield United in the next round.

A difficult season would end badly for the hapless Hatters though because they were relegated along with Chelsea and Carlisle United. They won 11 and drew 11 out of 42 matches, but that was not enough to save them and they went down with 33 points, one fewer point than Spurs.

"It was a shame we had to go down but the reality is we were a small club with a limited squad that was competing with bigger and wealthier clubs that had a lot of quality players," he lamented.

"We finished the season strongly but it was clearly a case of too little too late."

The following season in Division Two was when his English experience started to turn sour.

The club was struggling on and off the field. Alston, who never had an agent to look after his affairs, was still owed part of the $40,000 signing-on fee the club had promised to pay him.

He also fell out with manager Harry Haslam after an incident at training when he reacted angrily after a stoush with a new recruit. Haslam was not there but the trainer saw everything and 'reported' Alston.

"I was called in to the manager's office for a 'please explain'," Alston said.

"I thought the manager was on the young player's side and this annoyed me, which is when I told him there was no way in the world that I would get kicked and not retaliate. Things were never the same with Haslam after that meeting and I could see that my future with the club was up in the air.

"I was in and out of the team because I seemed to have lost favour with the manager, and the fact I was owed money forced my hand.

"I asked for a transfer and after a handful of matches into the 1975–76 season, Cardiff

City came up with a very attractive offer that included paying me the money Luton owed me. I put pen on paper and moved to Wales.

"Cardiff were in the third division but they had a number of famous players in their ranks, among them former Spurs' and Wales' centre-half Mike England. I looked at their squad and said, 'Geez, they don't have a bad team'."

In October 1975, Noddy and his family were on the move again. They packed their bags for the beautiful city of Cardiff.

The Alstons' football journey had taken another twist and Ninian Park was to be the player's new home.

Chapter 13
Career at a crossroads

Sometimes one has to take a step backwards to move forward, and this is precisely what Alston did when he decided to trade Luton Town for Cardiff City in late 1975.

The Australian World Cup star, who was still basking in the recognition of his eye-catching displays for the Socceroos in Germany's football fest in 1974, left the Hatters to sign for the Bluebirds, who were languishing in the English third division.

It would turn out to be an inspired decision for Alston who still regards his sojourn in south Wales as one of the most enjoyable and rewarding in his career—up there with his three seasons at Sydney's St George in the early 1970s. Not least because the Alstons' second child Debbie was born in the Welsh capital in December.

Alston's career at club and national level would take him to five continents, but playing for Cardiff was something special because the move west rekindled his passion for the game after a few turbulent times at Luton.

Falling out with your manager and being owed money by your club are a professional footballer's nightmare and Alston had to endure both in Bedfordshire.

On the other hand, Cardiff was like a breath of fresh air to the player who must have felt that at the age of 27, his career was at a crossroads.

The Bluebirds won promotion to the second division in Alston's first foray in Wales and the club capped a memorable season by winning the Welsh Cup and earning the right to play in Europe in the now defunct Cup Winners' Cup in 1976-77.

Alston did not have any Socceroos 'distractions' to worry about during his Ninian Park odyssey. He was able to fully concentrate on meeting his club's expectations. He produced some of the finest football of his career in Cardiff's colours, playing many matches, scoring plenty of goals and earning the adulation of the club's discerning fans.

"Cardiff were in 13th position when I arrived in late October," Alston said.

"It was a special time for me, and once again I was so fortunate to be able to bank on the full support of my new teammates.

"I trained in Cardiff for the first time on a Friday morning. It was a session organised just for me to check out the ground. I was given plenty of crosses from left back Clive

Charles, who used to play for West Ham United, and I headed the balls towards goal.

"On that very same Friday evening, I made my league debut against Chesterfield and, would you believe it, Charles sent over a diagonal ball which I controlled with my chest and before the ball hit the ground I volleyed it into the net.

"That was after only a few minutes. I scored another goal in a 4–3 victory so the home fans must have been delighted with their club's newest signing.

"The touring Wallabies' rugby team were playing Cardiff the next day at Cardiff Arms Park and came to watch us play. I would like to think that they liked what they saw. I got 24 tickets for the Wallabies' game from the Australians which I distributed to my new teammates. They were impressed."

Cardiff had a season to remember in 1975–76 and Alston played a key role in the club's success. He was a regular starter for the rest of the season that ended with the club gaining promotion.

They finished second behind champions Hereford United and ahead of Millwall. Alston crowned a top performance for his new club by netting the winner in Cardiff's final-day 1–0 victory over Bury.

But both Cardiff and Alston's exploits were not restricted to the league championship. After getting a taste of the FA Cup with Luton in the previous season, Alston got another bite at the cherry and this time he made the most of it.

In a first-round tie with Exeter City, he scored a glorious hat-trick in a 6–2 rout to become the first Cardiff player to score three goals in a single match in the famous competition.

"I remember that match very well … all my goals were headers," he said.

"It gave me a nice feeling, but I did not know that I had made history. I just enjoyed the game and was told about the record later.

"We had a good run in the cup. After beating Wycombe at home, we faced Orient away in the third round.

"On our way to the match, we stopped for lunch somewhere on the motorway. We all had a travel allowance whenever we were away and the boys had their customary fix of carbs such as toast and cereals, but I ordered a steak.

"Manager Jimmy Andrews went off his head when he saw me have that 'shit food', but I eventually scored the winner in a 1–0 victory and on the bus home the boss told me that from that moment onwards, I could order anything I wanted on our away trips."

Cardiff's run ended in the fourth round when they lost to Norwich City.

However, they would not be denied cup glory because there was also the Welsh Cup to play for. The quarter-finals paired Cardiff with Swansea City and after a goalless draw, Alston scored twice in a 3–0 win in the replay.

In the semi-finals, Cardiff defeated Chester 1–0 in a replay thanks to an own goal by future Wollongong City defender and captain, Chris Dunleavy.

In the final, Cardiff renewed their heated rivalry with Hereford. Their league match at Ninian Park a month earlier had drawn a huge crowd of 36,000 fans.

The two-legged final was marred by controversy after the first leg in Hereford ended in a 2–2 draw but the match was later declared null and void by the Welsh Football Association because the home team had fielded an ineligible player.

So the return leg became the new first leg and both teams played out a thrilling 3–3 draw in Hereford.

The second leg at Ninian Park was played the next day and Alston played his part in helping Cardiff to a 2–1 victory.

Cardiff's cup win meant they would represent Wales in the following season's Cup Winners' Cup, but they would have qualified anyway even if they lost the final. English clubs like Hereford, Chester and Shrewsbury Town that come from areas close to Wales used to be invited to take part in the Welsh Cup. But no English club who managed to win a Welsh Cup was allowed to play in the Cup Winners' Cup. That spot went to the highest ranked Welsh team.

While Alston was wooing Cardiff's fans with his goalscoring exploits, he was conspicuous by his absence in the Socceroos team.

After Rasic's controversial sacking, the national team was taken over by Englishman Brian Green.

Australia played six times against the Soviet Union in 1975 and more friendly matches in 1976 under fellow Englishman Jim Shoulder, but Alston was nowhere to be seen. He believes the federation was not too keen on bringing him over from Britain for friendly matches.

"I was keen to play, but I suspect it might have been too hard for the federation to organise and fund my travel to and from Australia," he claimed.

"I certainly was available. Why would I not want to play for my country? The club would have let me go because they could not do anything about it, but of course by going away I would have risked losing my regular spot after I came back."

His second season with Cardiff in Division Two started brightly.

Having won the cup the previous season, Cardiff was back in Europe and in a qualifying round of the Cup Winners' Cup, Alston helped the Bluebirds beat Switzerland's Servette on away goals to make the main draw.

Cardiff was pitted against Georgia's Dinamo Tbilisi.

Today, Georgia is an independent country but it was part of the Soviet Union at the time. Dinamo had won the Soviet Cup by beating Ararat Yerevan in the final in Moscow only two weeks before they met the Bluebirds.

International playmaker David Kipiani was the star attraction when Dinamo travelled to Ninian Park for the first leg, but it was Alston who stole the show 17 minutes from time with a well-taken goal that gave Cardiff a narrow 1–0 victory.

"I struck a volley from about 24 metres that went straight in. It was a cracker, an absolute gem of a goal," he recalled. "However I hurt my calf in scoring the goal and had to go off a minute later."

Alston's goal made him the first Australian player to score in European club competition.

Dinamo were too strong for Cardiff in the return leg in Tbilisi thanks to an inspired performance by Kipiani. They scored a comfortable 3–0 win to go through to the next round.

Playing in a communist country was yet another eye-opening experience for Alston, even though he had played in some 'strange' places in Africa and Asia throughout his career.

"They had a massive crowd behind them in Tbilisi but that was to be expected at that level of competition. It was a draining trip. We had to stay overnight in Moscow before going on a five-hour train journey to Tbilisi and arriving on the day before the match," he recalled.

"When we got there, everybody was offering us money for our jeans and our Western clothing. It was a strange experience. The food was a bit 'different' and our accommodation was rather unusual because we had to roll out our mattresses onto wooden beds, but to be honest I was used to that sort of stuff after my travels with the Socceroos, but some of the boys were saying, 'bloody hell' … it was a culture shock to them.

"It would have been nice of the authorities to let us change the roubles back to our pounds before we left … We got stuck with worthless money but overall the Georgians treated us wonderfully. They were lovely people."

However, the reality is that Alston should not have played against the Georgians. Two weeks earlier, in a League Cup match against QPR, he broke his toe and missed two league matches that Cardiff lost to Oldham Athletic and Notts County.

"I actually came back too early," Alston lamented. "Cardiff lost twice without me and I think they needed me to play. I wanted to get back on the field too but realistically we should have waited a bit more. I was stupid because I should have insisted and told the club that I was not right yet. I was not quite the same when I came back."

Many years after leaving Wales, Alston was pleased to learn that there is a substantial number of Cardiff City fans in Australia. "There is a Sydney-based supporters club and they call themselves Bluebirds Down Under," he explained.

"Barry Jones is a Welsh friend of mine who lives in the Illawarra and one day in 2005 or thereabouts he asked me to go with him to a function of the fan club in Sydney. I went there and no sooner did I walk through the door [and] they took me back to a chant I used to get all the time at Ninian Park. One end of the ground used to yell 'Alston' and the other would respond with 'Ooh, ooh'. When they saw me at the function, they stood up and did that again.

"I was touched because it brought back some beautiful memories. It also made me realise how well known I was. I was happy and honoured to go to a few more meetings."

Jones was confident of speaking on behalf of most Bluebirds' supporters when he described Alston as a "Cardiff City icon".

"Alston was Cardiff City's 'Ronaldo'," Jones said. "He was a very special player, the likes of which we had not seen before."

Soon after Christmas 1976, Alston's career took another turn when he received an offer to join Tampa Bay Rowdies, who played in the NASL (North American Soccer League).

The young competition was soon to be adorned by great players and household names like Pelé, Beckenbauer, Carlos Alberto, Cruyff and George Best who were all head-hunted by the money-laden league in the latter stages of their illustrious careers to give American football a popularity boost.

Alston was excited by the prospect of mixing it with those guys and taking up residence in sunny Florida.

"It all came about when Tampa coach Eddie Firmani, who had played in Italy for Internazionale, showed interest and this went on for a couple of months," Alston said.

"When the push came to shove, they contacted me on the phone although they were not supposed to and made me an offer that was very lucrative.

"Tampa also put in an official offer to the club and Cardiff agreed to a transfer fee of an equivalent of $250,000. This bloke from Florida then came over to snowbound Cardiff in white pants, checked jacket and slip-on shoes. We went for lunch and in a couple of hours I agreed terms with the club and signed the biggest contract of my career, which was for three years. I got a signing-on fee of $20,000 and I was to be paid $US1,600 a week if we won, which we would do quite often. I would never again see that sort of money."

Alston was about to discover America.

Chapter 14
Flying the flag for Australia

Football in the United States was going great guns in the second half of the '70s, a decade after the FIFA-recognised United Soccer Association amalgamated with the National Professional Soccer League to create the North American Soccer League.

In 1967, the two rival bodies decided to pool their resources and unite for the good of the game that seemed to be going nowhere, but it was seen in some quarters as a sleeping giant.

The first national competition kicked off a year later amid scant mainstream interest simply because soccer was not a major sport in America. It was a climate similar to the one that prevailed in Australia at the time.

If Australia's sporting culture was dominated by the widely followed Australian Rules, rugby league and cricket, in the United States it was gridiron, baseball and basketball.

The NASL was a semi-professional affair in its first years of existence and something needed to be done to save the stagnant competition. Then came the sensational acquisition of Brazilian legend Pelé, who signed for New York Cosmos in 1975, and everything changed.

Pelé's arrival—and that of West Germany's Beckenbauer and Brazil's Carlos Alberto later on—gave Cosmos and the struggling competition a massive credibility boost. The corporate world that had never wanted to have anything to do with soccer was suddenly scrambling for a piece of the action.

And the previously lukewarm (if not antagonist) media could not get enough of the only man to win three World Cups and the two star defenders who had captained their countries to global glory. Huge crowds were drawn by the magnetic appeal of Pelé and Cosmos at the Giants Stadium in East Rutherford and wherever they were in action.

Other ambitious clubs were forced to jump on the 'big names' bandwagon and in no time guys like George Best, Gordon Banks and Cruyff were lured by the mighty 'greenback'. They were given a simple but very important task: to give American soccer a much-needed shot in the arm and help the game reach its full potential.

By the time Alston joined Tampa Bay Rowdies from Cardiff in early 1977, the competition whose crowd average was less than 5,000 in its first years had gained so much popularity and credibility that the figure had jumped to just under 14,000.

Soccer was getting much better coverage in national newspapers and for the first time league matches were given considerable exposure by influential television stations such as CBS and ABC.

The game was moving in the right direction and it was a new world that suited Alston as he and his young family flew to Florida to chase their own American dream.

"Nearly every time I moved from one club or one country to another, I always went first and my wife Doreen did the packing and all the hard work, but this time we all went together to be greeted at the airport not just by club officials but also some supporters," Alston said.

"The Rowdies had some amazing people running the club and they looked after us very well from the very beginning. They put us up in a nice hotel in town until we settled into a three-bedroom condominium on a lake which was amazing. It had three swimming pools, tennis courts, games rooms and the lot, which was great for the kids. The place was a 20-minute drive from where we trained, which was handy.

"Two days after we moved into the condominium, Tampa coach Firmani took me to a car yard so I could buy a vehicle. I loved those big American cars and I bought a Buick station wagon which was a whopper. After I completed the paperwork and sorted everything, Firmani left me and I hit the road.

"The problem was I did not know where I lived, so here I was behind the wheel in a big city and not knowing my address. I tried to remember the way home but all I did was go on the wrong side of the highway and nearly cause an accident.

"I had no mobile phone then so I pulled into a cocktail bar on the side of the road and asked them if they could get in touch with the Rowdies. They tried to help me but they were very curious about my accent and all they wanted to do was find out where I was from. All I wanted was to go home.

"Luckily the club's executive secretary—a lady named Dale E Wellhofer—came out to show me the way home. From then on it was a little easier to get around but it was quite funny at the time, embarrassing even.

"Thanks to Dale, the club also paid for some hospital fees when my son Adrian bit his tongue after falling and hitting his chin while playing on the swings at the hotel. That was on our first morning in Tampa and we spent it in hospital.

"The club also footed the hefty bill for a plastic surgery on my son's forehead a few months later after he got hit by a swinging bat when he was playing baseball with bigger children. Thank god for the club's help because in America you just cannot afford to get injured or become sick. You have to pay for everything over there and it would have cost me heaps.

"Dale was just a wonderful lady, easily the best club official I had to deal with in my entire career.

"The Tampa area was beautiful, very much like the Gold Coast, and downtown Tampa reminded me of Sydney. The city is on the bay and it has a marina with lots of yachts and a waterfront with many bars and restaurants."

It took Alston no time to feel at home in a big city that enjoyed warm and sunny days almost all year round. His wife Doreen loved Florida's balmy weather and his son—injuries apart—had a ball in his new surroundings that were far more attractive than the ones they had left behind in Cardiff.

The Alstons found Tampa to be a place that was very easy to settle in because its laid-back lifestyle was very similar to that of Australia. From the football side of things, the NASL was thriving and gaining worldwide recognition and respect.

Tampa, who overcame Portland Timbers 2-0 in Soccer Bowl '75 (American soccer's version of the A-League grand final) to win the championship in their first year in the competition, were keen on the start of the 1977 campaign in the eastern conference in April. They once again would face the considerable challenge of their biggest rivals, Cosmos.

Each one of the 18 clubs in the competition had many foreign players—some of them household names like Beckenbauer and Carlos Alberto—who were enlisted at the same time as Alston.

"The clubs were signing famous players from around the world and others I had known from my days in Britain, so the league had a certain familiarity about it although I must admit the razz element within the game took me a bit by surprise," said Alston, who was the first Australian to play in the NASL.

"None more so than on the occasion of my home debut for the club. They used to have what they called 'tailgate parties' at our home games. They pulled down the tailgates of a few wagons and had food and drinks for the fans for a party in the car park before the game.

"I was picked up and taken to a helicopter pad in town and it flew me over the Tampa Stadium ground that had 33,000 expectant fans in attendance.

"They used to introduce players one at a time in America and I could hear the announcer saying something like 'and all the way from Australia, let's welcome Superoo Adrian Alston'—as if I had just flown in from Sydney—before the chopper landed and I could enter the field of play with my gear on and ready to go.

"It was one of several ways the club used to introduce us to the fans. Another was being transported to the ground in huge vintage cars. It was very unusual, very American and very beautiful."

Alston could not have hoped for a better introduction to his new club and its supporters because he scored twice in a 4-0 romp over Chicago Sting. "It must have been the helicopter," he quipped.

Tampa had a reasonably successful year and they qualified for the playoffs from the eastern conference thanks largely to a 4–2 victory over Cosmos in Tampa that drew a crowd of 45,000 fans. Tampa had never had such a big home crowd.

The first playoff match attracted a press corps from all over the world due largely to the fact that 'Kaiser Franz' was making his debut for Cosmos. It was televised live nationally and abroad, and Alston played the whole match.

The New York club had the last laugh though. They crushed Tampa's dreams with a 3–0 victory at a packed Giants Stadium before going all the way and winning the title with a 2–1 victory over Seattle Sounders in Soccer Bowl '77.

"We had a pretty strong attacking side and former England striker Rodney Marsh was the star of the team," Alston said.

"He is actually a very funny and genuine man. He came around to my place one day and we were hanging around at the pool and on such occasions when you're relaxing you get to know about people's lives. Rod told me stories of his humble beginnings and where he came from which reflected my own. He did not come from a big-money family … he was a backstreet kid from Hertfordshire who became a very good footballer.

"We tended to play with two wide men, Steve Wegerle and Derek Smethurst, who were both from South Africa, me as the main striker and Marsh just behind me. They called our attack the 'swarm' for Smethurst, Wegerle, Alston and Rodney Marsh.

"We were an attacking team and people liked the way we played. We drew strong crowds all season and when a big game was on, 40,000 people were guaranteed.

"The playing standard in a league that was full of foreigners was obviously very high, believe me. We also drew 1–1 with Roma in a friendly in which I scored direct from a free kick. And if you look at American football now, Major League Soccer is a great league and most stadiums are usually packed."

Alston said he was aware all along that Tampa had established themselves as a strong and ambitious club in their short existence. They were founded in 1975 and demanded excellence from their players, especially since they outlaid a considerable amount of money in a bid to compete successfully with 'moneybags' Cosmos.

Alston was paid handsomely for his services but the striker never felt he was under any extra pressure to perform. Pressure never got to him, anyway.

"To begin with, my wages were not over the top and by the time you bought a house, ran a couple of cars and other stuff, the money was not so great anymore," he said.

"Of course there were expectations, even on me personally. I was an international footballer who had played in the World Cup only three years earlier, so I had to meet the club's expectations … and I would like to think that overall I did that.

"But to be honest, I was not 100 per cent satisfied with my first season in America mainly because I never am. I always came across as a happy-go-lucky chap but that does not mean I was always happy. The reality is that I wanted more from that season.

"For example, I would have preferred our wingers to go to the byline and cross the ball more often so I could get on the end of things—they did not call me Noddy for nothing—but that is not how we played. We usually built our attacks through the middle and they played the ball to feet and so on. Football was changing and more goals were coming from forwards who played deep than from out-and-out strikers like me."

Alston did not enjoy the same high profile of some of the mega stars that made up the competition, but he was glad to notice that the written and electronic media began to pay more attention to this long-haired 'Superoo' from 'down under' as the season wore on.

With each strong performance—he scored seven goals and made three assists from 17 matches—his popularity among the fans and the media went up a notch.

And with Tampa having a strong season on the eastern seaboard, good publicity from the media was never lacking.

"I never had any problems with the media, so I dare say they were happy with the way the team and I were playing," Alston said.

"Tampa used to hold lunches just for the media the day before each home match and on the occasion of Cosmos's visit, I was invited to speak at the lunch after a light training session. Pelé, Beckenbauer and striker Giorgio Chinaglia were there on behalf of Cosmos while Tampa was represented by English midfielder Len Glover and me.

"I told the gathering that I was the only Rowdies player to have played against the two legends Pelé and Beckenbauer, and I said, amongst other things, 'Pelé, this is one time I've got to say it, Beckenbauer is my all-time favourite player'.

"Which was fine … however at the end of the lunch I had a picture taken with the five of us and we put our arms around each other, but Pelé did not put his arm around me.

"No wonder Pelé never sent me a Christmas card."

Like anybody else, Alston was deeply dismayed to learn of the great man's death in December 2022. The Brazilian legend passed on after losing his battle with cancer.

"Pelé was the best forward in his time and nobody could discredit that," he said. "Actually, make that the finest forward of all time.

"What a player and what an ambassador for the game. He reinvented the striker's role because he could do everything, not just be a target man.

"I feel incredibly proud to have played against him on three occasions."

Chapter 15
Noddy answers SOS call

Things were not going too well for Johnny Warren's Canberra City in the first season of the Philips Soccer League in 1977.

The new club from the capital was languishing at the bottom of the table with two wins and 10 defeats in the first 16 matches. At just over the halfway mark of the 14-team competition, Canberra was looking down the barrel of relegation.

Coach Warren was forced to think outside the square and that is when he made a desperate call to a dear friend in a last-ditch attempt to save his sinking ship.

The Socceroos legend knew that 1974 World Cup teammate Alston was just the player who could instil some confidence in a demoralised side and help it climb the table and retain its position among Australia's elite.

Alston and his Tampa Bay Rowdies club were headed towards the business end of the NASL season when he received an urgent SOS call from his old mate. Or rather a series of SOS calls, to be precise.

"Johnny wanted me to play for the Canberra club in the second half of the season and he rang me constantly ... I felt an obligation to help him and his battling team but there was a little problem ... I was a Tampa player and the NASL was still in full swing," Alston recalled.

"Johnny was a very close friend and he needed a hand. I wanted to help him of course, so I asked the club if I could go away on loan for a short period and they agreed to loan me out to Canberra, probably because they were going to save some money for a few weeks.

"They also may have said 'yes' due to the fact that Johnny rang the club directly asking for me to be released. The club and I agreed that I should leave in July and report back for pre-season in early 1978.

"I travelled to Australia on my own. Doreen and the kids went back to Preston for a few months so they could catch up with our two sets of parents."

Alston played his last match for Tampa on 19 July when he came on as a substitute and helped himself to a goal in a 4–1 home win over Las Vegas. Tampa was inclined to leave him out of that match altogether because he was flying out the next day, but he told the coach, "Put me on the bench in case I'm needed."

Four days later, Noddy played his first match for Canberra against Adelaide City in Round 17. He would end up with 10 full matches until the end of the season, scoring three goals.

It was not a huge tally by his standards, but two of the goals he scored on the road may have safeguarded Canberra's status in the top tier. He came up with a late equaliser to earn Canberra a 1–1 draw at South Melbourne and scored a last-gasp winner that gave Warren's team a 1–0 win over Brisbane City.

Canberra finished the season in second-last spot, two points ahead of Mooroolbark who were relegated to Victoria's state league.

"Those vital goals allowed Canberra to stay in the national league, so I was delighted that Johnny got what he wanted," Alston said. "Can you imagine the all-round disappointment if the team from the capital city were relegated after all the hullabaloo?

"I thoroughly enjoyed playing for Canberra although it must be said that throughout my career I loved playing anywhere, in any division and at any level. I was never going to be the type who enjoyed getting heaps of money for sitting in the stands and playing once a month. I loved the game too much.

"Canberra had a very young side with two 17-year-old fullbacks in Danny Moulis and Steve Hogg. Johnny sought to boost the team's experience by bringing in Tony Henderson, 23, and goalkeeper Ron Tilsed, 25, who were both playing in South Africa.

"You could see that 'Hendo' was a fine player and he would become a Socceroos' star for several years, while Ron was a member of the England under-18 team that won the 1971 European Championship. Ron and I hit it off immediately and we are still close mates.

"Ronny used to come up with some incredible mischievous pranks. One day we were involved in the match of the day which meant we would be on live ABC television across Australia. He gained himself a neat sponsor for the day which involved him wearing a bright white goalkeeper's jumper with a car manufacturer's name on the front. He kept the tracksuit on for as long as possible so as not to alert anybody, and just before kickoff he whipped off his top and there it was … his sponsor's name on national television.

"That caused quite an uproar among the game's suits and he got in trouble later on but he didn't care … he got his $1,000, which was exceptional money those days."

Alston had certainly made a valid contribution towards the club's safety, but his good deed for one of his best mates hit him where it hurts—in the hip pocket.

"When I came here, I soon discovered that Canberra were not in a position to pay me the money I missed out on by being away from Tampa," he explained.

"I got paid only a fraction of what I was getting in Florida, so by helping a friend

I actually lost money.

"Johnny of course must have been embarrassed and was very apologetic. He tried to compensate by getting a couple of newspapers to hire me to write some weekly columns on the league for a few hundred dollars, but it was not enough.

"I knew almost straight away what was going to happen because the Canberra club had a limited budget and its lowly position in the league did not encourage too many people to come and watch our home games. But I played on anyway for Johnny."

Alston admitted he also came to Australia on the assumption that he was going to get picked for the latter stages of the Socceroos' 1978 World Cup qualifying campaign.

The national team had fallen into the hands of Englishman Brian Green since the shock dismissal of Rasic after the 1974 tournament in West Germany.

The Socceroos played six matches against a touring Soviet Union side in 1975 and in mid-1976 fellow Englishman Jim Shoulder took over the national team with the task of assembling a competitive side for the World Cup qualifiers.

After a series of meaningless friendly matches in 1976, the Socceroos started their qualifying campaign in 1977 by winning a round-robin against New Zealand and Taiwan.

The Australians were then pitted in a final group comprising Iran, South Korea, Kuwait and Hong Kong. They played their first four matches in Australia but did not take full advantage of the home factor.

Shoulder's troops started well by beating Hong Kong 3–0 in Adelaide but came a cropper in the next match in Melbourne when they fell 1–0 to their old rivals, Iran.

The Socceroos then gave themselves a lifeline in their next match in Sydney with a 2–1 win over South Korea, thanks to two goals by new striker John Kosmina.

Alston was called into action in the next match against Kuwait, but a shock defeat in Sydney was a body blow to the team's hopes of reaching their second straight World Cup.

"The Australian team had already played three games at home when I was picked and with four away fixtures yet to come, the chances of qualifying were not looking great," Alston recalled.

"I played in midfield against Kuwait and we lost 1–2 … that defeat probably sealed our fate.

"To make matters worse for me personally, Abonyi was booked twice along the way and he was supposed to be suspended for one match but it was my name and not Atti's that was put forward for suspension.

"I was shocked to find out that I was suspended when I had not even been booked. By the time we found out what had happened it was too late because we were already in Kuwait City preparing for another qualifying match against the Kuwaitis and our federation was not too keen on fixing the mistake because we were already virtually eliminated anyway. So they just let it go. We lost 1–0.

"I played against Iran in our last qualifier in Tehran and we again lost 1–0 in front of 100,000 people. Little did I know then that I would not play for Australia again. Iran won the group and went on to play in the finals in Argentina.

"After the Socceroos' matches, I joined up with my family in England and we had a lovely Christmas together.

"Tampa had chosen London for their 1978 pre-season so we moved there from Preston for a while until we all went back to Florida for the start of my second season."

After the Socceroos' disappointing exit from the race to reach Argentina, Alston was ready to concentrate on his club football in America, which is where his bread and butter came from.

What annoyed the striker who had given everything for the team was not necessarily the elimination, but the meek manner of the Socceroos' surrender.

World Cup regulars Schaefer, Richards, Warren, Mackay and Buljevic had quit international football after 1974, while Utjesenovic ended his green and gold career in late 1976.

Stalwarts like Wilson, Curran and Rooney stayed on and played in most of the qualifiers for '78, but Abonyi became a fringe player and Reilly lost his regular spot.

The team had many fresh faces, among them goalkeeper Allan Maher, defender Col Bennett and centre-forward Kosmina, while '74 fringe players Williams and Ollerton had become regulars.

"I did not know many of the new players in the Socceroos' set-up. Several of the ''74 blokes had quit international football and only a few were still hanging around," Alston lamented.

"Everything had changed from 1974. There was not much that could be done about the retirements, and even those who stayed on were nearing the end of their careers.

"But having said that, it just seemed a very different set-up from the one I was used to. Too different. It was like going from day into night.

"I just felt that the team had far too many changes and could not jell quickly enough to give our qualifying campaign rivals a shake. I'm not going to point the finger at anybody for our failure to qualify for Argentina.

"Okay, Shoulder was not very experienced because I don't think he had coached any club teams before he got the national job, but he was not the main problem. I believe there were too many inexperienced newcomers who needed guidance that just was not there … or there was not enough of it, anyway.

"I was surprised to see Atti on the bench for some matches. Here was a vastly experienced player who would have been invaluable to the younger players in the team. I also remember Rooney and Reilly being on the subs' bench which did not make any sense to me. I was on the bench too.

"It just seemed to me that the (partly enforced) revamp was too drastic and a bit too early. If Rasic had carried on, he would have built on the '74 success and not sacrificed most of the team at the same time. He would have brought in new faces, for sure, but only gradually.

"I tell you, some of the players who quit after the 1974 World Cup would have stayed on if the federation had done the logical thing and retained Rasic. I have no doubt about this.

"But planning ahead was never Australian football's forte and we often paid dearly for this. Just look at how the world's major countries like Germany and the biggest club sides operate and you'll see why they are so successful. The changes they make are gradual and certainly not wholesale."

The much loved Socceroos were in for a lean period after their 1974 peak. After Germany, it would be 32 long years before the Australians would get another taste of World Cup football.

Chapter 16
An American dream is crushed

They were three words that brought Alston's world to a crushing end and made him realise that, at the young age of 30, his football career was over.

"Son, you're finished," was the brutal assessment of a Harley Street specialist when asked to examine his shattered right knee in mid-1978.

The Socceroos' World Cup striker was not completely surprised by the verdict, but the moment he was hit with the grim reality that he could not play football anymore felt like he had lost a big part of his life.

Alston was looking forward to another successful season in the NASL with his go-ahead club Tampa Bay Rowdies. Fresh from a lovely Christmas with their families in Preston, the Alstons were back in Florida and the striker was as ever keen to get started after a stint with Canberra in the inaugural Philips Super League.

Alston had also played a small part in the Socceroos' attempt to reach the 1978 World Cup when he turned up for the green and gold in four matches in late 1977 during Tampa's off-season.

The Australians were soon up against it after crashing to home defeats to Kuwait (1–2) and Iran (0–1) in a final round-robin comprising five teams. By the time Alston joined the group, elimination was seen as only a matter of time.

The Socceroos duly failed to qualify for the finals in Argentina so there was to be no second World Cup for him.

In the first match of the 1978 NASL championship on 1 April, the Rowdies scored a home 2–1 win over Memphis Rogues in front of 26,233 jubilant fans at Tampa Stadium. Alston helped himself to his first goal of the season.

Things were looking very promising.

The club was eager to go further than their previous campaign when the Rowdies lost to Cosmos in the first round of the playoffs while Alston, not being one to rest on his laurels, was determined to add to his tally of seven goals and three assists, especially since he was renewing his predatory partnership with former England striker, Marsh.

However in the second match of the season against New England Tea Men eight days later, disaster struck.

After an innocuous tackle, the likes of which you see plenty of in any match, Noddy hurt his knee on Foxboro Stadium's AstroTurf and had to go off.

"It was quite early in the game versus New England and I was playing against big centre-half Larry May, who was an ex-Leicester City defender," Alston recalled.

"He was very strong and aggressive, but I was used to those sort of defenders even though I was not a tough player at all. I was a ball-playing forward, and copping tackles from behind was common. I would have loved to be playing nowadays and knowing you are not going to get hacked from behind all the time.

"We were playing on Astro Turf and the defender came in from the side to tackle me. I planted my right foot, went to play the ball with my other foot and he hit me on the knee of my locked foot—grass is a bit better to play on than Astro because it allows you a little more give—and I snapped my cruciate. It was so loud it sounded like a rifle shot.

"I knew straight away that it was serious but I was not thinking of [my] cruciate ligament ... those days we rarely heard of such injuries. The only other person I knew who had cruciate ligament damage was Warren and he came back to play in the World Cup.

"After the game, we flew back from nearby Boston to Tampa via Miami and by the time I got back home I was in extreme agony. On one of the flights they had to cut up the side of my pants because the knee had blown up and the pressure was killing me."

The Tampa club did not seem to appreciate the full extent of Alston's injury and he was urged to 'run it off' via individual exercises at training. It would be the worst advice he would ever get.

"I did 14 weeks of training and running on my own but my condition did not improve and eventually they sent me for an arthroscopy which determined that I had a torn cruciate ligament. Both sides of the bone were ripped," he said.

"I was really disappointed with the club because it had taken them that much time to establish the extent of my problem when it could have been done much earlier.

"I had a nasty feeling that my days at Tampa were numbered because I was in the country on a sports visa. My fears were confirmed when the federal authorities informed me that since I was not playing, I had to leave America and I had three months to do it.

"My contract was terminated and the club paid me out. I had to sell my house, which I did and we went back to Cardiff because the club had expressed an interest in re-engaging me. I had a couple of training runs with Cardiff because I was hoping they could fix me up, but I was struggling and I just knew I was in trouble.

"Cardiff did not give up though and they sent me to a specialist in London. He checked me out and came back with the news I had been dreading all along. But when it came, I felt like I was hit by a sledgehammer. He said, 'Son, you're finished'. That was it, just like that. My professional career was over.

"My heart sank because I realised there and then that I was finished as a professional player at the age of 30. It was the lowest of the low.

"The injury was deemed unrepairable those days and no surgery was performed. So I just said to myself, '*I'll have to wear it and get on with life.*'"

The Alstons were faced with a dilemma that they were not expecting so soon: what to do with the rest of their lives after Adrian was ordered not to play professionally anymore.

Alston then took his family to Preston. "The devastating news I got from Harley Street meant we had to completely start our lives again," he said. "It was yet another move for us, but Doreen took all the drama in her stride and handled it beautifully as she always did."

When they were living close to their folks in the north of England, Alston was asked by his brother Alec if he would join him in a business venture.

"My brother already had a place in Fleetwood and he was looking at buying a bigger hotel on the beach in Blackpool, which is only a 30-minute drive from Preston.

"He wanted me to go into business with him and go halves. I outlaid half the money and we got into a massive mortgage to acquire a 30-room hotel which was a full-board type of accommodation, not just an ordinary bed and breakfast.

"We went through the Christmas period, which is traditionally very busy. The venture, however, did not work out and a few months later in 1979, I got a job with Preston council. They were building a sporting complex outside Preston North End's Deepdale ground and they wanted me to manage it.

"In the meantime somebody in Florida asked me if I could go to St Petersburg, which is close to Tampa, and coach the town's soccer team called the Thunderbolts that played in the second division.

"So the next minute I was back in America. I coached there for a while but I had another problem with our visas so we had to leave the country again and return to England, which is where I got a job with a health club in Preston."

If 1978 was a bad year for Alston the footballer, 1979 became even worse and more distressing for Alston the father.

His seven-year-old son Adrian contracted the rare Perthes disease. It is a condition that affects children aged between three and 11. Blood supply to the head of the thigh bone is disrupted which causes it to deteriorate.

"It became a hip problem. He used to play football for a local team in Tampa and by halftime he'd start limping and we'd be at home and he'd be crawling on the floor," Alston said.

"We took him to several specialists and one of them told us that he needed special plastic callipers to be wrapped around his legs. They were designed to make his feet a metre apart with a metal bar across to stop him from closing his legs.

"He had that for 18 months but it was the only way that could enable the bone to grow properly. It was a terrible time for me and for Doreen. Thankfully by then we were back in England and we had family support.

"It was the new low point of my life. You tend not to worry about yourself and get on with it when something happens to you, but when something horrible like that happens to your children you don't know what's around the corner.

"I never cried so much in my life. To see him hobbling down the street was distressing. One day the schoolteacher rang up to tell us they could not find Adrian. He was up a nearby apple tree, his friends helped him up and he was hanging upside down.

"He had this amazing spirit and he was into everything. On another day, I went to pick him up from school and he was playing in goal in the school yard. He could not move his feet of course because of the metal bar and the kids were kicking balls at him. One time, he let himself fall on the ground and he missed the ball and I cried. It was the worst time, absolutely horrible. Thankfully, he recovered and today he is fine. And he still loves his football."

At the start of the 1980s, Alston the ex-footballer was able to reminisce on some exhilarating moments of his career that started on the streets of the northern English town of Preston and took him to the bright lights of the World Cup.

His career had its highs and lows, but throughout his playing days he never lost his zest for the game and for life. In the end, he was just grateful for the opportunity to make his childhood dreams come true.

Alston made many friends during his uplifting journey but some mates are more special than others. There is no doubt about what he regards as the most satisfying aspect of his career.

"Because of all my teammates, coaches, supporters and the friends I made, nobody could buy that. Of course I was totally satisfied with what we achieved because I regard the amazing period I spent with the Socceroos as the absolute highlight of my career," he said.

"We were a true family. We travelled together for months at a time as a group of 30-odd people that included coaches, physios, doctors and so on.

"Nothing compares to the special bond I established with the Australian national team and the players who wore the green and gold jersey with pride, honour and determination. Every one of us pulled in the same direction and we all got on well together. We still do, half a century later.

"Guys like goalkeeper Jim Milisavljevic, for example, hardly ever played a game but he never made a fuss. What a wonderful person he was.

"Being a member of that group of incredible people was like a gift from God … to be able to do what I did from where I came from in Preston was amazing. It is quite incredible, to think that as a kid from a little town I got to a stage in my life when many people knew who I am.

"To take all that away from me would be a disaster.

"If football was my life, the Socceroos were my lifeblood.

"From a playing perspective, I was satisfied too but I always tried to be better at whatever I did and achieve more, but it was not meant to be."

Alston's playing career was finished but his liaison with Australian football was anything but.

Chapter 17
Warren and Wilson, the born leaders

Alston knew straight away that something was up when his old mate Johnny Warren walked through the front door of the former striker's villa in Unanderra, south of Sydney.

His Socceroos teammate used to live in nearby Jamberoo on the NSW south coast in 2004.

And one fine day Warren rang to tell Alston he was coming around for a chat.

"He brought a bottle of wine and I felt straight away from his body language that he was not bringing any good tidings," Alston recalled.

"We were sitting in the backyard and he said to me in a morose tone: 'I've got something to tell you, Noddy … I've got cancer … and I'm dying.'

"He explained the tragic situation but I was not listening properly because I was in complete shock and trying to comprehend what I had just heard. I just burst into tears which is when Johnny told me, 'Don't ever cry for me again, Noddy, please. Promise me'.

"I said, 'I promise you, Johnny, I won't do that' … I lied.

"It was a most devastating period in my football and personal life … Johnny was a great teammate and an even better friend.

"He died shortly after at 61 years of age. His funeral in Sydney was obviously a very sad occasion for the '74 Socceroos … he was the second to leave us after Mackay."

Warren and '74 captain Peter Wilson would become two of Alston's best friends after he met them in the late 1960s, not long after the Preston lad started playing in the NSW First Division.

The two were completely different characters with wildly disparate personalities, but they both struck a chord with Alston.

Warren was a deep-thinking university graduate who was destined for bigger things in the game he loved with passion, while Wilson was a music-playing, fashion-conscious eccentric who walked away from the game when he finished playing.

Alston crossed paths with forward Warren for the first time in a pre-season trial match in 1968. He met defender Wilson for the first time a year later when he and South

Coast supremo Birch picked him up at Sydney Airport after he had quit Middlesbrough for Australia.

"I first met Johnny during my third match in Australia in 1968. South Coast were at home against St George in a trial and I got two goals and Johnny scored three in a 4–4 draw, I think," Alston said.

"Johnny was already a high-profile player at that stage and a local reporter asked me what I thought of his stellar performance.

"I said bluntly, 'Who's he?' to which the reporter replied, 'He's the guy who's just scored a hat-trick'. I said, 'Well, I scored two'.

"I did not know who the Saints players were and as far as I was concerned, Johnny was just another player from another club … a very good player, by the way.

"My introduction to Willy was somewhat different. Birch had been surprised to see just a little boy—not the big centre-forward he expected—turn up when he welcomed me to Australia a year earlier, but Willy's arrival was the opposite. We met this six-foot tall, blond defender who had long hair down to his shoulders and who was immaculately dressed. He had this beautiful brown leather jacket, a black silk shirt and flared black trousers. He was the epitome of the English fashion of the 1960s. Birch said to me, 'Bloody hell, look at this!"

Alston cannot speak highly enough of the impact both players left on him as a footballer and a person … and on the game in Australia.

Wilson took to Australian football like a duck to water and would go on to captain the Socceroos at the 1974 World Cup in West Germany, while Warren the thinker would become a coach and forge a career in the media when his playing days were over.

"I always appreciated good players irrespective of race, colour, background, religion or whatever," Alston said.

"Straight away, you can pick those who love the game or the ones who are just going through the motions. Johnny and Willy loved football with a passion.

"Johnny was St George and NSW skipper. For a while, he captained the national team before he got injured. He was a well-educated man and had great leadership qualities. It was obvious even then that he would go far. He was interested in coaching courses while he was still playing and the media career he made for himself later came as no surprise. His views were highly respected.

"Johnny was an all-round great player. He had two good feet and it was a privilege to play alongside him for the national team.

"Willy was a different type of player. His qualities were equally remarkable. He was a top defender but he also could come out of defence with the ball because he was deceptively very quick.

"During matches, you could not fully appreciate his mastery of the ball because he could not show all his skills in a defensive position … it would have been too risky.

"But I tell you, at training he was amazing—controlling the ball with ridiculous ease, putting it between people's legs all the time and basically dominating proceedings.

"He would have made a classic holding midfielder, but of course the Socceroos were already excellently served in that area by Richards. To be fair, Willy could have played anywhere from midfield backwards.

"Willy and Johnny were both good leaders on the field—always vocal and never back-pedalling for anybody because they were winners and it was always encouraging to have such players in your team.

"However to be perfectly honest, when it comes to leadership and you're in a team, you do not wait for your captain to lift the team when things are not going well … you've got to bloody do it yourself. Football is full of non-captains who were big stars and great leaders.

"The two were different players of course, and their characters were poles apart, but they had one thing in common: their ability to switch off from everything and concentrate on their football.

"Like myself, they were dedicated and prepared to make sacrifices to give themselves the best chance of realising their ambitions.

"But while football for Johnny was his life because he had nothing else, Willy had other interests such as music and of course, his clothes."

The influence exerted by Warren and Wilson was not limited to the football field.

The Socceroos went on many trips abroad in their manic quest for football's holy grail. Never was the need for strong guidance more pressing than on those long trips to faraway lands where they had to contend with unfamiliar conditions, and sometimes, hostile environments.

When cool heads were needed, there were no better people to have around than Wilson and Warren, and for different reasons.

"They were just two members of the Socceroos squad but Johnny, the sensible one, was always very careful, eloquent and to the point in his speeches after games and made you think, while Willy, who was a bit of a joker, always provided light moments to ease any tension that might have existed within the group in some of the difficult assignments we faced away from home," Alston said.

"Willy did not speak much. One night we were at a function somewhere and he picked up the microphone and said, 'I would just like to thank the inventor of the venetian blinds because without him, it would be curtains for us all'. That was it. We looked at each other. We kept quiet for a while, then we all started clapping. We had no idea what he meant.

"At another smaller function, he was given a microphone. He put it in his pocket and just mimed for five minutes. That's Peter Wilson for you."

Alston, as a person who knew the two very well, is in an ideal position to dismiss once and for all the malicious rumours that marred the build-up to the 1974 World Cup. These rumours would not go away even after the tournament.

Many supporters wondered: did Wilson and Warren get on?

The rumours and innuendo started when Wilson was given the Socceroos captaincy after previous skipper Warren tore his ACL in 1971.

When Warren came back into the Socceroos reckoning after 15 months out of the game, he expected to regain the captaincy. But by that time, Wilson had established himself in the role and Rasic opted to retain the status quo.

Hence the rumours of a rift between the two key men with very strong personalities.

"I know them both very well and I can categorically say that any talk of a rift is absolute rubbish," Alston explained.

"People just spread those rumours and journalists gave them oxygen just like they did in politics.

"It was wrong and factually incorrect. Somebody in the background was trying to make up a story out of nothing ... a story that Johnny Warren hated Peter Wilson because he was the captain and not himself.

"It was all bollocks. ... and that's official. They got on as well as anybody else in that '74 squad. Believe me, there was no problem between the two.

"The people on the outside who claimed that the two did not get on were never in the dressing room, they were not amongst us and they did not travel with us, so their claims did not count.

"It was not an issue within the squad either. From a personal point of view, for example, I could not give a shit who was captain as long as I was in the team."

The captaincy became a highly sensitive issue in the weeks leading up to the World Cup. Matters took a nasty turn when a newspaper article questioned the wisdom of having an Englishman captaining the Australian national team.

It was a direct criticism of those who gave the captain's armband to English-born Wilson and not to Warren, who was a local hero and as true-blue an Aussie as can be.

Alston is adamant that Wilson was not affected by the newspaper article, such was his dedication to the team's colours and his determination not to let anything distract him from the job at hand.

"He would not have been upset at all because there were so many media stories going around at the time that I don't think he even read the papers," he said.

"I can tell you, Willy was never going to be offended by something like that.

"When he finished up, however, something went on with him. He got upset with the way he was treated by his last club APIA after he got injured. He became disillusioned with the game and he just walked away from football, never to return.

"Willy did not suffer fools gladly and the reason he did not want to have anything to do with football is because he was wary of its bureaucracy. He could have tried his hand at coaching, but I suspect the reason he refused to do so is because he would not have taken kindly to being told what to do by some board member with little or no knowledge of the game.

"Willy was a different man and his own man, and he was like no other player I knew. He was a weirdo. Nothing surprises me with him.

"I'll give him this. When we played for South Coast in 1969, every Friday after work in the steelworks he used to come to stay with Doreen and I in our place in Corrimal until Monday morning. We had some lovely times together and that is probably when I got to know him really well. I roomed with him when the Socceroos went on the world tour of 1970 which was the trip my usual roommate Abonyi missed because he could not get time off work.

"We had some hairy moments though. One night we went out for a few drinks at a club on the south coast with Doreen and a companion of his," Alston recalled.

"He was dressed up and looked a million dollars, but his long blond hair caught some unwanted attention when he went up to the bar to get some more drinks.

"These two young blokes gave him a girl's whistle, but he ignored them. The whistles continued after he joined us at our table and they even called him 'Shirley', at which point Willy rose and fronted them, asking them, 'Is there a problem?'.

"Before we knew it, Willy decked one of the young men, punched the other on the face and when the barmen intervened, he hit him as well.

"I don't think we ever went to that place again."

They had known each other for only a short time and Alston was beginning to understand that—on or off the field—you just don't mess with Peter Wilson.

Chapter 18
Lifting the gloom

Adrian and Doreen Alston and their two young children were at the crossroads of their family life in the wintry months of northern England in 1982.

Adrian senior's career had been savagely terminated by injury and Adrian junior was recovering from the debilitating Perthes disease.

Living in Preston, despite the fact they were close to their families, would not have been the Alstons' first choice of residence. But life can deal you the sort of cards that ruin your best plans and make you unsure of what lies ahead.

Sometimes you need someone or something to show you the way and give your life a clearer meaning and purpose.

The Alstons got that 'sign' when young Adrian, who was then 10 years old, came up with a simple yet loaded question to his parents.

"When we came back from St Petersburg in America in 1979, I started working for the Trimline Health Club in Preston," Alston said. "They were a big company and had a few centres in the north of England. They were very nice people and I ended up managing the place. It was a good job, but Australia was really where I wanted to be.

"One day young Adrian got up and came into our bedroom with his pyjamas on and was wiping the window from the condensation. You could not see outside. It was grey, miserable and freezing cold.

"And he said to us, 'Why are we not in Australia?' I looked at Doreen and she looked at me, and it just clicked straight away. I answered him then and there: 'We're going'. That was it. Adrian had made up our minds and we said, 'That would do us'.

"It was a hard time for us as a family with my son having the Perthes disease and my football career being over because of the ACL. I wasn't unhappy with our lot, but Australia was really where I called 'home', and my son's simple remark sounded very logical and it was all I needed.

"The bottom line was the future of our children. It was not in England; it was in Australia.

"Within a week, I rang Wilson and Birch and told them I needed somewhere to stay because I was going to Australia the next week. I booked my ticket and told Doreen to sell our house. We had a mortgage to pay off. We never got in front of our repayments because we never lived in a place long enough.

"Doreen and the kids stayed behind in Preston and it took her about six months to sell the house. I returned to the south coast and worked in a car yard for my former South Coast coach, Harris. I did a few other jobs too."

Alston could not play football anymore, but his love of the game and his yearning to stay involved meant he would have welcomed a coaching job in Australia with open arms, although he knew he was not experienced in that side of the game.

And with a family to support, Alston realised he could only do a coaching job on a part-time basis because there just was not enough money in the game.

Football in Australia had not taken full advantage of the success of Rasic's Socceroos in 1973 and 1974. A national league was launched in 1977, but five years down the track, many clubs were struggling financially with poor crowds and scant exposure, and most players were part-timers.

In late 1983, Wollongong City president Laurie Kelly offered Alston a three-year contract to coach the battling club in the 1984 national league.

The Wolves had finished second last in the table the previous season and they were looking to bounce back. However, they had to do it on the cheap and make do with locally based players as replacements because several senior stars had left the club in the off-season.

Nonetheless, it was an opportunity for Alston to make his mark on the game in Australia as a coach after doing so much to enhance its image as a player.

It would also be a stiff challenge.

"I took over when seven players from the first team had been sold in the off-season," Alston said. "They went to Sydney because the Wolves club could not afford to pay them and I ended up with a locally based team. Four or five of them were under 20 years of age.

"So we were expected to challenge the big clubs like Sydney City and Sydney Olympic, who had Kosmina and Marshall Soper leading their respective attacks, with a bunch of players from the local league, basically.

"One of the Wolves players transferred was ball-playing winger Phil O'Connor, who was a second-grader at Luton when I was there in 1974–75. O'Connor could never get a senior game [at Luton] and when I spoke highly of him with manager Haslam, I was told, 'He's not ready yet for the first team'.

"Later on in the season, remembering what Kelly had told me when I was with Fleetwood, I urged O'Connor to move to Australia because the game 'down under' would suit him perfectly. I told him, 'You'll do well in Australia, taking on defenders'. He came to Balgownie before joining the Wolves and was so successful, he became an Australian international.

"Anyhow, I knew the Wolves job would be a massive challenge for me, but I loved football too much and I wanted to remain involved at any level. You meet good players and others who are not so good, and if you can help them improve in a small way it means so much.

"So I saw the job as a window of opportunity for me to give something back to the region that had provided me with a platform from which I launched my international career. The Illawarra meant a lot to me and it still does."

But was Alston, the footballer who was never afraid to gamble, prepared for the coaching job with all the planning and pressures that go with it? Was he ready to deal with the myriad of problems, the likes of which he never had to face as a player?

"I picked up a lot of things along the way by observing and listening to coaches," he said. "However we are all individuals with our own ideas and I would not do what some of them did.

"As a coach, I tried to organise my team's style in a way that suited the players. Why would I ask my team to play out from the back when my goalkeeper cannot pass the ball, for example?

"You cannot say you want to play in a certain way when you do not have the type of players to do so. That is a bit stupid. I always tried to accommodate the players' style, not the other way round."

Despite his good intentions, Alston could not save the Wolves from the ignominy of the wooden spoon. The Wolves won five and drew five matches out of 28 in the northern division.

In 1984, the league was divided into two conferences based on geography in a bid to cut travel costs. At the end of the season. Alston resigned from the job, claiming interference from the board had made his position untenable.

"I had a lot of arguments with the club because some of the people that employed me thought they knew more than me," he claimed. "Again, there was no money for the players and for me they always came first, so at the end of the season I said, 'Enough is enough', and I quit.

"However, I should add that I did not walk away because we were not successful. That sort of thing did not bother me too much. I just would not accept all the bullshit from behind the scenes. Essentially, you had non-footballers telling footballers what to do."

Yet his coaching baptism of fire would serve him in good stead later because the frustrating stint with Wolves had opened his eyes to the complex nature of the position.

"Coaching is harder than playing, much harder," he said.

"You are not just coaching and looking after the players, but you also have to manage things that are unmanageable like dealing with injuries and suspensions over which you have no control.

"You also have to deal with people from behind the scenes—usually committee members—who ruin everything by their lack of understanding of the game.

"Coaching early on was very difficult and a learning curve for me, but later on it became less difficult because I had more experience and I could better understand how things work in management."

Alston's stint with Wolves produced an interesting anecdote for the statistics buffs. In round 18 of the competition in July, Wolves were away to Sunshine George Cross in Melbourne and a goal down with 15 minutes to go.

Alston chose the occasion for an unexpected 'comeback' when he came on for young Alex Bundalo—whom he had introduced to the first team at the age of 16. It was his first senior competitive action since that fateful day in Foxboro six years earlier when he damaged his right knee while playing for Tampa.

"I registered myself as a player quite often when I coached even though I could not play," Alston said. "I used to love to have a kick for half an hour or so with the youth and reserve teams.

"We were getting beat 1-0 by Sunshine and I ended up putting myself on and we managed to grab an equaliser from striker Glenn Fontana, who is still a great friend of mine. So we came away with a point."

His first coaching job may not have ended well, but it made him appreciate the knowledge and expertise of his own coaches, Arok and especially Rasic.

Arok of course was Alston's coach at St George while Rasic was his mentor at the Saints and Socceroos. He learned a lot from two men of whom he cannot speak highly enough.

"Arok and Rasic were by far the best coaches I had in my career," he said. "I learned more from those two than from any other coach, more so Rale because I had him as a club and national mentor.

"But Arok was a super duper manager as well. I just thought they were a couple of jumps ahead of the other ones like Haslam (Luton) and Firmani (Tampa).

"They were forward-thinking and never afraid to change their minds when things were not going according to plan. Other coaches stubbornly stick to a game plan even if it is not working. They just wait and wait. That's not the way Arok and Rasic operated.

"So I learned from them that there is no point in being intransigent and sticking with your original game plan because circumstances change and you should react accordingly, the sooner the better.

"Take today's football, for example. It has become a trend for coaches to replace three players on the hour mark. It is as if they say, 'If everybody else is doing it, I'll do it too'. Arok and especially Rasic were their own selves."

As a forward who enjoyed 'doing his own thing' and trying to create havoc with his blistering pace and unpredictable dribbling, Alston fully appreciated the value of letting his forward players be themselves without burdening them with too much tactical instruction.

"I was fairly easygoing as a coach," he explained. "I used to give players a lot of freedom. I would never stifle those who could create things in the opposing penalty box.

"Freedom is the best way to get the best out of the players, particularly if they are forwards. They must know that it is okay to make a mistake as long as they are not afraid to try things and improvise.

"You see many players pass the ball very quickly because they are afraid of losing it. That is not right and I hate it. It is not the way I played and it was certainly not the way I wanted my forwards to play.

"I found in my first forays into coaching in Australia that many players were too scared to be successful. 'Just go and do it and enjoy it, come what may,' I used to tell them."

Alston's best time as a coach was just around the corner.

Chapter 19
Turning back the clock

The Alston-Abonyi partnership that captured the imagination of thousands of Socceroos' supporters in the mid-1970s resurfaced in the humble surroundings of Illawarra football more than a decade later.

Alston and Abonyi played a key role in helping the Socceroos reach the 1974 World Cup and the two strikers were deployed alongside each other by Rasic in two of the matches in the finals in West Germany.

Much water had passed under the bridge since the Socceroos' tussles with East Germany, West Germany and Chile.

Alston went on to forge a career abroad before he was forced to quit the game when he tore his ACL in the United States in 1978.

Abonyi stayed in Australia and carried on for a few more club seasons. He played a peripheral role in Australia's failed 1978 World Cup campaign before turning his attention to coaching.

After finishing up with Wollongong in 1984, Alston was not on the scrapheap for too long—those of his pedigree seldom are—because when his assistant Terry Hurley got the senior job at second tier Illawarra club Corrimal Rangers, he asked him to join him for the 1985 season.

Meanwhile, Abonyi was appointed Rockdale Ilinden coach.

"Corrimal were in the second tier of the region's football and saw Hurley as the man to strengthen their attempt to gain promotion to the Illawarra Premier League," Alston explained.

"Terry signed up with Corrimal and then asked me if I could join him. My time with Wollongong had its unpleasant moments, so I was only too happy to join the Rangers. We agreed to be joint senior coaches and I was looking forward to a new challenge."

That was when the old Socceroos' buddies crossed paths again.

"Atti would have been 39 in 1985 and he was coaching Rockdale at the time," Alston said. "I asked him if he could come and play a few games for us. I told him, 'If you sign for me, I'll sign too'.

"He had retired and not played competitively for a number of years, but was happy to come down as long as we obtained permission from his club Rockdale. He lived in Engadine, one of Sydney's southern suburbs, so it was a short drive for him.

"He did not train with us, but played about 20 games and scored something like 17 goals. I could not resist the temptation of turning the clock back. I came off the bench with 15 minutes to go on several occasions just to revisit our Socceroos' glory days by playing together at the top end of the pitch. I am a hopeless romantic and I just could not help myself.

"I probably played in a third of our league matches and every time I played, Atti and I enjoyed ourselves immensely … just like we did in the good old days. Atti was a ball player and he used to attract special attention from unscrupulous defenders and when he thought he was being fouled too much, he would nutmeg his much younger opponents, pick the ball up, give it to them then say, 'Sorry'. Cheeky bugger.

"Okay, it was Memorial Park in Corrimal not the Volksparkstadion in Hamburg or Berlin's Olympiastadion, but Atti and I had an absolute ball for old times' sake. Playing alongside him again after so many years, even if for just 15 minutes, was unbelievable."

Incidentally, Alston and Abonyi were opposing coaches when Wollongong met Sydney Croatia in the national league a year earlier. On that occasion, Alston's Wolves beat Abonyi's Croatia 2–1.

Corrimal won promotion to the Illawarra Premier League in Alston's first season and a new chapter in his coaching career was about to unfold. "Terry left the club after the first year and I was handed over the sole reins of the senior team for 1986," he said.

"I was excited to be given full responsibility for coaching Corrimal's football club. I was living in Mangerton then, but the Corrimal suburb held a special place in my heart. It meant a lot to me because I regarded Corrimal as my hometown … I've always seen it that way. It was where I stayed when I arrived as a young single from England in 1968 and where Doreen and I lived after we got married.

"The [Illawarra] Premier League was obviously more challenging and we never won anything. Corrimal was a steady family-type club that did not have a great deal of money, yet I savoured the experience of working with very nice people who trusted and respected me. I was free to work without interference and for this reason, I never had any problems with the Corrimal club.

"My grandsons go and watch Corrimal play occasionally and seven or eight of my players came to a recent reunion to celebrate the birthday of local football identity, Peter Dent's wife Beryl. Dent was a senior club official when I signed for the Rangers."

After serving the Corrimal club for six years—five as head coach—Alston decided to take a one-year sabbatical from football to concentrate on his full-time job. He had been employed with the Disability Trust since 1986 and wanted to go to university to improve his position.

"Two years after signing for Corrimal, I got a job with the Disability Trust, a non-profit organisation that started off with six people but now employs 1700 people across New South Wales," he recalled.

"I wanted to obtain a degree in social services and that meant travelling to Charles Sturt University in Wagga often.

"So in 1991 I decided to have a year away from football after my six seasons with Corrimal. I did not try to cut corners. I quit Corrimal in order not to put pressure on the club by not turning up now and again."

Noddy did not complete his degree because, after twelve months away from it, the lure of football was too strong to resist. He was missing the game and especially the regular interaction with players and football people in general.

"Port Kembla made contact with me in 1992 and offered me the position of head coach of their club which was in the Illawarra's second tier," he said.

"I was at the Warrawong Shopping Centre waiting to pick up my wife who was managing a ladies' clothing store. I was approached by a gentleman who introduced himself as Vince Raschilla and we started talking about football.

"He then told me he was involved with the Port Kembla club and said to me it would be awesome if 'somebody like you could coach us'. He however conceded he was sure that big-name players like me would not lower themselves to coach in the Illawarra's second tier and they would cost too much anyway.

"I said, 'But you didn't ask me'. We kept talking and at one stage I asked him if he would like me to be their coach and he said, 'Of course'. We did not discuss money at first, but we clicked because he sold me an interesting project for the club, and in a week, I was head coach of Port Kembla.

"We won promotion to the Premier League in our first season and I would end up spending 13 years with the club. In that time, we won five premierships—which I considered real championships—and seven grand finals in the Premier League.

"On four occasions, we won the double and during my period there we won every trophy that was available.

"Port Kembla, which were an Italian-based club, were very professional, supportive and forward thinking, so that made my job a little easier. They never flinched at whatever I demanded as coach.

"One day, I asked the club to replace the old balls we used at training with new quality balls, the type which were used in proper matches on Saturdays. "They said, 'no problem', and the next day we had all these expensive balls that would have cost the club a little fortune.

"As with Corrimal, my stint with the Port Kembla club was very satisfying and enjoyable.

"It was obviously the most successful time in my coaching career. They also made me Illawarra coach for representative matches against sides from Canberra and Newcastle and I'm proud to say my teams were never defeated."

Midway into his 13-year stint with Port Kembla, Alston and Dr Corrigan (who had saved Ray Baartz's life all those years ago after a 1974 World Cup warm-up match for the Socceroos) would cross paths again, many years after they had both retired from Socceroos' duties.

After having fully recovered from Perthes disease, Alston's 22-year-old son Adrian was playing centre-forward for local club Lysaghts in 1994 before he joined Port Kembla the following year.

"At first, I did not want to get involved with his football and sign him because I did not want people to accuse me of nepotism," Alston explained.

"But Adrian insisted on coming to Port Kembla to play reserve grade because he wanted me to guide him. I told him I would sign him but he would not play up front, but as a fullback. It just happened that my left back in first grade broke his leg and I started playing Adrian there.

"Two years later, he suffered a nasty injury around the pelvic area. It was diagnosed as osteitis pubis, which is an inflammation around the centre of the pelvis."

Young Adrian was in constant agony and, in a scenario reminiscent of his Perthes disease a decade earlier, his worried parents took him to many specialists. But they were not getting any closer to finding a cure until Adrian senior chose to give his old soccer federation doctor a call.

"Dr Corrigan was retired but he was more than happy to see our son," Alston said.

"He asked Adrian to lie on the floor, stand up and do some exercises, and all it took him was about 15 minutes to give us his verdict. He told him not to play football for 18 months and after that he'll be back playing.

"Honestly, 18 months later in 1999, Adrian's recovery was complete and he started playing again and that's when he won a few more trophies with Port Kembla—he played in and won five grand finals all up—until he retired in 2001 to join the police force."

Adrian junior had improved so much in his new role of fullback that he earned representative honours with the Illawarra. "All this after Dr Corrigan's intervention, for which we are all grateful," Alston said.

Alston was dubbed the Illawarra's most decorated coach after his triumphs at Port Kembla and his achievements inevitably caught the eye of his former club Wollongong City, who were now in the state league.

His arguments with the club from 1984 were still fresh in his memory but he was prepared to give the Wolves another go. "The Wolves came for me again because of my success with Port Kembla and they made me a very good offer," he said.

"This was well before the end of the 2004 season and Port Kembla knew about it and that I was likely to leave the club. The club was fine with this and we got to the grand final and we beat Picton Rangers 4–0."

However, his second stint with Wolves in 2005 would provide him with the same problems and frustrations he had to put up with two decades earlier.

"I had to take the offer really because it was substantial, but once again I had no luck coaching," he lamented. "It was the same old story. The club was not run properly— some players were not paid on time—and it just did not work out for me. In hindsight, I must admit that I twice went to Wollongong at the wrong time.

"I ended my coaching career with Bulli, where I spent six years. I was glad to touch base again with Kevin Love, who was a youth player at South Coast when I arrived in Australia and who was now a committee member and for whom I have the utmost respect.

"Bulli made three grand finals and finished runners-up in the premiership on three other occasions. We did not win trophies but, hey, I made so many friends there and that made me a happy man.

"I had that feeling of fulfilment with the Corrimal, Port Kembla and Bulli clubs I worked with."

When his time with Bulli was up, Alston quit the game altogether in 2012 and was able to concentrate on his full-time job of helping people with disability in a so-called independent living program.

Alston could look back and cherish the beautiful memories of a career that many children can only dream of. He had his dark moments, of course, but the overriding sentiment he will take from a career in football is the sheer satisfaction of being regarded as someone who was prepared to have a go in his quest to make his childhood dreams come true.

He is also blessed with the knowledge that along the way he made friendships that have lasted a lifetime, not least with the members of that special group of part-time Socceroos who played in Australia's first ever World Cup.

"You're always proud of your achievements of course, but what fills me with the greatest pride is the fact that I have made so many friends along my football journey that started in Australia in January 1968," he said.

"I am a proud Australian and I relish the fact that people respect me for what I did for my country. Not putting you on a pedestal or trying to drag you down … just making me feel I am part of the football family."

There was never ever any doubt about that.

Chapter 20
A new life after football

Alston never imagined that life after football that centres on his job as a Disability Trust officer would be as rewarding and uplifting as when he played for Australia at the highest level of the game.

Working with intellectually disabled people not only provides him with the kind of personal satisfaction afforded only to a select few but also has made him a better and stronger person.

Alston took up the job in the second half of the 1980s and has grown to love it so much that at 75 years of age he has no intention of giving it up any time soon.

"It's just a great privilege to work with such people who have an intellectual disability," Alston says.

"It's been wonderful to see the progress they've made over the years in terms of the difference in their quality of life and the strides they've made.

"I never thought I'd find something that means so much to me after getting injured and having to retire from football.

"It is as rewarding and satisfying as when I used to bang them in on the football field. The only difference is when I used to score for club and country everybody knew about it because it was in the media but the work I do with these lovely people goes largely unnoticed.

"I just love my job which allows me to get close to these people and through trust and understanding teach them to be independent with support, without which they would struggle.

"I would like to think that I have made life much easier for many people but I tell you working with them has made me a better person too.

"At the moment, for example, I am working with several people who have a mild to moderate intellectual disability and live independently.

"I help them with their lifestyle in such areas as shopping, paying bills, medicals, hygiene and looking after themselves.

"Some of them cannot fully understand what is going on around them and this is where they need to be protected more than others.

"As I said before, I started off in sport and recreation but my job later evolved into what I do now, partly because at 70 I was having trouble playing indoor soccer."

His association with the Disability Trust happened by chance.

"One day a gentleman named Arnie Olbrich called me and asked me if I could go to a nearby indoor soccer centre and deliver a coaching session to a group of intellectually disabled footballers," Alston says.

"He said 'I know who I'm talking to—you are Adrian Alston, the former Socceroos' striker–and I'm just someone asking you for a favour'.

"I said, 'Of course, I'll do that,' so I went to the venue and this guy had about 15 men with a mild disability who were playing in open competition against non-disabled people.

"I enjoyed the 'tutorial' there and I got to meet Olbrich who turned out to be one of the nicest and most generous people you could ever hope to meet. He was roughly my age and he was playing with them.

"Two days later, I was glancing at the newspaper and I saw this Disability Trust ad for the position of sport and recreation officer. I thought to myself, *Geez, doing sport and rec would suit me,* so I applied and I went to the interview, and would you believe it, this bloody Olbrich was on the Trust's panel.

"He just looked at me and asked if I was sure I wanted to do that job and I said, 'I thoroughly enjoyed myself interacting with those people'.

"They gave me the job and I got stuck into it with a passion. Helping such people was an uplifting experience. One of the most satisfying moments would come in the Barcelona Olympics in 1992 when four of our players were selected for the Australian Paralympic squad.

"So that is how my career with the Trust started. And I'm still there. It has been a massive part of my life."

Retired Disability Trust chief executive Margaret Bowen, who got the ball rolling in 1987 soon after Alston joined, cannot speak highly enough of the footballer-cum-support worker.

"Adrian impressed me immediately with the way he supported people with disabilities," Ms Bowen said." He was encouraging, empathetic and most of all, a lot of fun. Many of our people with disabilities idolised him and they still do today.

"I recall a celebrity football match in which Adrian played alongside our people with disabilities. It would have been easy for him to dominate but he knew he was a supporter and was happy to set up the ball for our clients to have a shot on goal. We won and the celebrations were understandably huge because it was the first taste of victory for a group of people who are usually marginalised.

"Adrian is now the longest serving employee of the Trust and retains his good humour, quick wit and a sense of fun that is greatly appreciated by management, colleagues and clients."

Alston is still grateful for the support he has received from Ms Bowen over more than 30 years.

"For her, what was most important was the welfare of the clients. They always came first and that is what impressed me the most about Margaret and I am sure I can speak for the whole Trust," Alston says.

Alston's love affair with the Trust continues and it is for this reason that, health permitting, he intends to keep going till he is 80.

Chapter 21
Alston scores his greatest goal

Adrian Alston the footballer is the first to admit that he could have done things differently in his colourful career, but he has no doubt that he can look back with fondness on the day he set his eyes on a teenage girl who would enrich his life in a way he could not imagine.

The Socceroos' World Cup striker, who is now 75, is happy with the way his life has panned out. But having his two children and their spouses plus five grandchildren around the table for dinner once a week is all he and his wife Doreen need to feel a sense of pride and accomplishment.

Football gave Alston plenty of beautiful and lasting memories, but nothing beats the immense satisfaction of having a close-knit family around you all the time.

"With the benefit of hindsight, I could have been a bit smarter and done a few things differently over the years, but the bottom line is it has worked out for the best," Adrian said.

"I've got a beautiful wife who has supported me from day one and a loving family and what makes it special is that they all live nearby. Adrian and his wife Richelle have triplets Sam, Zander and Amber, while Debbie and her husband Des have two girls Holly and Emmy. We have them all for dinner once a week, which is great. My brother Alan and his wife Linda also live very close to me."

Alston and Doreen met when they were both teenagers who were working for a book-binding company in Preston in the mid-1960s.

It took no time for the whirlwind romance to become something more 'binding' and serious because both knew very early in the piece that they were meant for each other.

"We were both working at Askews, a book-binding place. I was 15 and Adrian was 16," Doreen recalled. "It was very quick and we started going out soon after we met."

Doreen's family liked what they saw in the dashing young man from the very beginning and they welcomed him with open arms. "They used to feed me and I would spend a lot of time at their place," Adrian said.

"I remember walking 10 kilometres to get home late at night because I often missed the last bus. It was worth it though because we knew we were on to something special."

The relationship was going great guns when Adrian, who was playing non-league football for Fleetwood at the time, one day told his girlfriend he was thinking of moving to Australia in early 1968.

He told her he was offered an opportunity of a six-month loan to NSW club, South Coast United.

To say that the proposal caught Doreen by surprise would be an understatement, but she typically took the development calmly as if Adrian had suggested they go to the movies. She said she was fine with it because it was only for a short time anyway.

"He just said to me he was going to Australia, just like that," Doreen recalled.

"I said 'okay' ... it was not a permanent move and he was going to be back after six months, well before Christmas. But then a few months after he left Preston, Adrian asked me to come over and I followed him 'down under'.

"We were a working class family and I did not have the money ... the one-way return air fare was more than six hundred pounds. [But] both my parents thought it was a wonderful idea, so I emigrated as a 10-pound Pom and I had to stay in Australia for two years because if I went back before that I would have had to pay the full fare.

"We treated it as an adventure and I did not think that Australia was that far away, but the reality is I did not get to go home for another five years.

"I went to live with [South Coast supremo] Trevis Birch in Corrimal which is where Adrian was staying.

"Times were different [in] those days, so we slept in different rooms.

"Very soon [afterwards] we got married and Trev gave me away and his two daughters Jackie and Robyn were my bridesmaids. They were like my sisters and I still see Robyn every month."

Adrian would go on to achieve some incredible goals ... playing in the World Cup, earning a professional contract with Luton in England's then First Division and becoming the first Australian to both score in European competition and play in the United States.

And as he moved from one place to another to further his blossoming career, he was fortunate to have a partner who fully understood what football meant to him.

Juggling his football and family lives was therefore not difficult and Adrian has no doubt about who was responsible for that.

"It was the easiest thing in the world because Doreen made it easy by sacrificing everything for me," Adrian said.

"She has been there from start to finish and put up with a lot of shit.

"I have made mistakes and at times our relationship was rather strained. But Doreen knew what football meant to me and she was happy to allow me to concentrate on my career.

"I always aspired to better things after I kicked the first ball in anger in Australia. Coming here was not the end of the road for me. When I saw NSW play, I thought to myself, *Why can't I be in that team?* It was the same thing with the national team. I was not Australian at that stage and I was imagining going back to England eventually to see where my career would take me.

"I had a good wage with South Coast, but manager Kelly kept telling me, 'Get a job, get a job and save some money' so [that] I could have two wages, but no way. All I wanted was to train and play.

"I never had a good attitude for work ... until after I quit football, of course. And during my time as a player and a coach, Doreen was always there throwing her full support behind me, first as a wife, then as a mother. She was never the sort of person to push herself forward ... she just looked after the kids and got on with it without any fuss."

Doreen said that despite the constant moving from one place to another, it was not hard to be a footballer's wife, mainly because she essentially saw Adrian as a husband first, then as a footballer.

"I think I managed it properly," she said.

"I never saw myself as a footballer's wife, I was just a normal wife who looked after the house and the children and let Adrian concentrate on his football. I miscarried three times before I had Adrian in 1972 and I was heavily pregnant with Debbie when we moved to Cardiff In 1975, so I just had to adapt to circumstances."

Of course, the Alstons' married life was not always a bed of roses.

In 1978, Adrian incurred a dreadful knee injury while he was playing in America and his career was dramatically cut short, a business venture in Blackpool with his brother Alec went pear-shaped and for several months, two worried parents were faced with their son's rare disease.

Those times were certainly not happy days for the go-ahead couple, and it was their stoic refusal to be beaten by adversity that saw them through.

"I think that time was the worst in our family life," Adrian recalled.

"I had no income because Tampa had obviously stopped my wages after paying me out. My green card was not valid anymore because I was not playing, so we went back to England where I got involved in the hotel venture with my brother that did not work out, and to top it all off, we had to deal with our son's Perthes disease. It was a horrible existence, especially for the kids, to be honest. After three months, we came back to Australia and we have lived here ever since."

Alston is more than satisfied with what he achieved as a footballer, especially when he remembers where he came from.

"As a player, I emerged from St Peter Street in Preston to rub shoulders with some of the world's greatest players," he said proudly.

"To play against even one of such superstars as Pelé, Beckenbauer, Best, Carlos Alberto and Bobby Moore was something. To play against all of them—some more than once—is truly special."

Chapter 22
The 'dream team'

Alston had no hesitation in naming the entire 1974 World Cup squad as his own 'dream team'.

He played with some fine and famous players in his career, but he is adamant that his association with the heroes in green and gold will always be one of the highlights of his eventful life.

The part-time players stole the hearts of a nation by reaching the finals in West Germany against all the odds.

At times during their qualifying campaign, they looked like they were gone. Particularly when they were two goals down to Iran in Tehran and had to deal with an hour of intense pressure to get through.

Or when they again were two down in their last qualifying round against South Korea in Seoul but came back to earn a draw and a decider.

They survived on both occasions because they were able to fall back on a quality that said everything about who they were and what they stood for: a never-say-die spirit that ran through the whole squad.

Alston, who is a 'member' of Australia's Hall of Fame, is also named in Australian football's 'Team of the Decade' for his exploits in the 1970s.

The team in a 4-4-2 formation is: Reilly; Utjesenovic, Schaefer, Wilson ©, Curran; Mackay, Rooney, Richards, Baartz; Alston, Abonyi.

"Being inducted into the Hall of Fame and picked in the Team of the Decade makes you very proud, especially because you are in the company of some of Australia's finest footballers," Alston said.

"It was a reward for what I achieved by coming to Australia, and as far as I'm concerned, there could be no higher accolade.

"During my time here, I was regarded as the best striker so all this made it all official, I suppose."

Noddy is happy to describe in his own words what made the '74 Socceroos such a special group of footballers who are still loved and respected by hundreds of thousands to this very day.

Here are the 21 players that made the trip to Germany plus key man Baartz who missed out on the experience of his career due to a serious injury suffered two months before the tournament kicked off.

Atti Abonyi (St George)

Atti was my favourite player of all time and a bonus to play alongside him. He was a wonderful goalscorer and we hit it off after we played together in my first international match against Greece and he scored the winner.

He was obviously a wonderfully talented No. 10 and Manchester United were so interested in him when they played in Australia in 1967 that they invited him to join the party for the rest of the tour.

We were roommates for many years and I regarded him as a true gentleman. There was no finer person than Atti.

We were very close friends and we were still in contact with each other regularly until he died this year. His passing was not unexpected but still very hard to take because Atti meant a lot to me. I was so glad I drove up to Coffs Harbour to see him just before he passed.

Ray Baartz (retired)

Once again, we are talking about a top striker who played superbly for his club—St George and Hakoah—and for Australia.

He scored many goals in his career for club and country and it was very disappointing that he missed out on the World Cup.

It was always difficult to play against players of his calibre. He was highly respectable as a player and a person.

Branko Buljevic (Footscray)

Branko was a rare breed because of his sweet left foot. He was skilful on the ground and very strong in the air.

He was also a funny man and great to have around. On our trips abroad, he used to come into my and Atti's room every night and tell us stories about where he came from in what is now Serbia.

Rasic loved Branko and he used to call him, Atti and myself 'the three gangsters'.

Ernie Campbell (Marconi)

Ernie was a very talented and quick forward, and he had to be otherwise he would not have been in the squad.

He was a very valuable squad player in the World Cup, yet before the tournament started he got some unexpected recognition when a South American commentator picked the best-looking team in the tournament and he got in ahead of me, which pissed me off!!

Joking apart, he was an important impact player. You could not call him a sub because he was a member of the squad. We were a team of 22 players and it did not matter what number you had.

Col Curran (Western Suburbs)

He made me laugh all the time. 'Bunny' and I used to sit together at the back of the bus, cracking jokes and what not. He used to like a beer after a game. He was great fun.

On the pitch, he became a fierce competitor. I love left-footers and Col was one hell of a player. He was strong, a great tackler and a marvellous crosser.

Players like him are considered superstars today.

Dave Harding (Pan-Hellenic)

Dave was a very pleasant English midfielder who was laid-back and unassuming, not a loudmouth like me.

He was very skillful and I tended to appreciate him more when I played against him at club level.

Jimmy Mackay (Hakoah)

One of the greatest of them all. He proved his status by playing nearly every game in our '74 campaign at an exceptional level.

He scored the goal that got us to the World Cup, but I used to say that since I was the top scorer in that campaign, I took us to Germany, and everybody had a laugh.

Jimmy, who died in 1998 at 54, was more than that one goal, much more. You would not think he was working hard but he read the game beautifully without having to run himself into the ground like a mad dog.

Another thing he did regularly in 50-50 tackles was let his opponent get the first touch then pinch the ball off them. He was incredibly smart.

Allan Maher (Sutherland)

Allan was second-choice goalkeeper in Germany but he became the No. 1 for the next (1978) campaign.

'Spider' was tall and skinny and he starred for his club—Sutherland. I played against him many times and you always thought you might split him in half if you collided with him. I remember him as being very brave.

Gary Manuel (Pan-Hellenic)

Gary was a stocky and very strong centre-forward who could hold up the ball very well.

And the fact I was able to start as the main striker in the World Cup at the expense of such an exceptional young player who was very intelligent made me feel very proud.

I knew that I had to perform because we had strong back-up.

Jim Milisavljevic (Footscray)

One of football's nice guys who could not say a bad word about anybody. He was third-choice goalkeeper in Germany and hardly ever played, but he went about things professionally and helped everybody.

I spent some time with Jim when the '74 squad members went to Hong Kong in 2013 for a reunion marking the 40th anniversary of our qualification.

That was the time we could reminisce on what went on in Germany and on him sitting on the bench but feeling proud just to be there. He was a lovely man. He passed last year.

Peter Ollerton (APIA)

I'm quite proud that as a Preston boy like me, we made it all the way to the World Cup together.

Peter was very tall and formidable in the air. He will be best remembered for the goal he scored against Uruguay when we beat them 2–0 in that ill-fated match in Sydney just before the World Cup.

The goal in a breakaway put Peter on the map as a feared striker, but he would become a very good coach in Victoria.

Jack Reilly (Hakoah)

I played with Jack at both club and international level. He was a very agile and reliable goalkeeper who went about his business without any fuss. He had a very good World Cup.

Jack was probably the smartest one amongst us and he was heavily involved in business in the financial sector at the time. He is very quiet and some might say he does not mix a lot, but for me he was a studious, very interesting and highly intelligent man.

I got on quite well with Jack and one day after the World Cup when I was playing for Luton, he came up to me before a game to say hello. How beautiful was that.

Ray Richards (Marconi)

Awesome: that's the only way to describe Ray. He was often given the toughest assignment in the team ... marking the opposition's best player.

I will never forget the match we played against Santos in Sydney in 1972. He was given the unenviable job of man-marking Pelé and he did it very well without committing one single foul.

He was clever and tough and had a fantastic throw. When we had throw-ins in the front third, they would become as dangerous as corner kicks and I used to love staying at the back post and attacking the ball near the penalty spot.

We are still great friends and I will bet that every Christmas morning, the first person to wish me all the best will be Ray.

Jimmy Rooney (APIA)

The 'mighty mouse' was a workaholic and would run all day.

You just had to have such players in your team because he was the type of midfielder who gave everything and supported you all the way.

He would come up to you as fast as he could when you were holding up the ball, to keep the attack going.

We had a great squad and Jimmy was a big part of it.

Ivo Rudic (Pan-Hellenic)

Ivo was an unused substitute at the World Cup but he took it all in his stride.

Having Wilson as a contender for the sweeper's role was always going to be a stiff challenge for the Split-born defender.

He never got to play for Australia but hats off to him, he never whinged. He was a very nice man who unfortunately passed on in 2009.

Manfred Schaefer (St George)

What can I say about Manfred? I played with him for many years at St George and with the Socceroos and I'm glad I did not have to play against him.

He was one of the fittest players I had ever seen and one day I remember we as a group were tested for our heart rates. We did a few laps and while our rate went up to over a 100 beats per minute, his remained a constant 50. It was hardly surprising because the 'milkman' used to have somebody drive his truck and he would run behind the vehicle, get the milk box and drop it off.

He always gave his best for his country and with him and Wilson at the centre of the defence, we knew we were in good hands.

His passing in 2023 was a very sad moment for us.

Max Tolson (Safeway)

Max was the toughest player I have ever played with or against. He would die for you on the field which is what he did for us all in that famous match versus Iran in

Tehran in 1973.

He had a great left foot and could head the ball well too. He was essentially a midfielder but he could play anywhere in the top half of the field.

Luck deserted him in Germany. We were playing a five-a-side indoors in the days leading up to our first match versus East Germany and he went to kick the ball but instead hit the radiator and broke his toe.

He did not tell anybody and when the team doctor came to check on him, he told him, 'Don't tell the coach' because he desperately wanted to get some minutes in the World Cup. He made the bench but did not play.

Doug Utjesenovic (St George)

A fantastic former OFK Belgrade defender who played centre-half for St George, but right back for the Socceroos.

Rasic brought him to St George from Footscray in 1971. What a signing!

Doug had this special ability to whip in crosses behind the defenders. I scored one of my two goals in the qualifier against Iraq when I got on the end of such a cross from the right from Doug. He used to do it constantly.

I used to call him 'McQueen' because one night we were in a club in Japan and the lady behind the bar called him 'Steve McQueen'."

Johnny Warren (St George)

Johnny was 'Mr Motion', always on the go. We became very good friends early in the piece, starting from the NSW team in 1969 before we went on to bigger things with St George and the Socceroos.

He was one of my idols because he could really play. He was our own 'special one'. He loved the game and he sacrificed everything for football, football and football.

He was the most one-eyed football man that I have ever known. He passed in 2004.

John Watkiss (Hakoah)

John is another super player who grew up with Warren in the same street in Botany, Sydney. They played their junior football together.

He was the perfect allrounder … he sometimes played up front for Hakoah and as stopper for Australia, and he was so consistent. He never played a poor game … I never saw him play badly anyway.

John was always one of the best players on the park and someone I had a great deal of admiration for.

Harry Williams (St George)

Harry was a very fast defender and could hit a powerful shot with his left foot.

I had a 'problem' with him, because whenever he got anywhere within 35 metres from goal, he would have a crack ... and I wanted him to pass the ball.

Harry was a wonderful and quiet lad, and nothing seemed to faze him.

I remember a training session we had in Manchester before we played City on our world tour of 1970 and it was raining, snowing and absolutely freezing. Harry had his tracksuit on and would not take his hands out of his pockets.

Rasic told him to 'take your hands out of your pockets' but he could not take the conditions and he just walked off. For the rest of our stay in England, he never got out of his bed.

Peter Wilson (Safeway)

Willy was a fabulous and unbelievable player for whom I had the greatest respect and admiration.

He was a magnificent sweeper but he could play stopper just as well too. He had everything anybody could ask from a defender.

I hated playing against him on the few occasions St George faced Marconi. What a bloody nuisance! Willy and I were very close. Doreen and I are in fact the godparents for his son.

Chapter 23
The long road from Germany to Qatar

Alston is not the sort of person to beat about the bush when it comes to offering an opinion on the game he loves with a passion.

Ask him any question on any aspect of football and he'll give you an honest and direct answer. No cliches, no platitudes, no sitting on the fence.

Shooting straight and telling it straight have always been the Socceroo star's hallmarks on and off the field of play, and age has not changed him one bit.

So when he was asked where the much-loved 1974 Socceroos would rank in Australia's national team hierarchy since the national team started their liaison with the World Cup, he was typically forthright about his views.

"You cannot possibly judge teams from different eras, full stop. But I will say this: if we as part-timers or semi-professionals had the same amenities, the same opportunities and the same level of professionalism of the more recent Socceroos, none of us would have remained in Australia because we would have ended up playing overseas … all of us, not just me," Alston said.

"I'm convinced about that. I'm not saying that they would all have played in England, but they would have landed in Europe for sure.

"A few of the squad had businesses here so they probably would not have gone, but the rest would have jumped at the opportunity to play professionally in Europe. And they would have got chances to go overseas because they were all very good players.

"And of course, they would have become even better performers if given the opportunity to be professionals."

After ending his blissful relationship with the green and gold in 1977, Alston did the next best thing by fervently supporting his beloved Socceroos in their subsequent campaigns to reach the game's holy grail.

He would follow the team as often as possible and rejoice in their triumphs and despair in their losses just like any of the hundreds of thousands of supporters around the world.

Like anybody else, he also has strong views on the national team's constant search for respectability at home and abroad. For example, even after all these years, Alston still cannot digest the Socceroos' failure to beat Iran in the final playoff for a place in the 1998 World Cup.

The Australians were minutes away from reaching the World Cup in France when they led the Iranians 2–0 late in the second leg of the final playoff at a packed Melbourne Cricket Ground. The side coached by Englishman Terry Venables had earned a 1–1 draw in the first leg in Tehran and goals in each half from Harry Kewell and Aurelio Vidmar put them in complete control of the tie before Iran stunned the 85,000 crowd with two late strikes to go through on away goals.

"That team had really good players who played well and their football was exciting to watch," Alston said. "It was devastating to see them miss out because I was convinced we would make it.

"We old Socceroos from 1974 were invited for the game and I said in an interview on the eve of the match that the home factor would make things very difficult for the Iranians.

"I knew from experience that there is a huge difference between playing in Tehran and at home in such do-or-die clashes.

"The Socceroos were flying for the first hour of the return match and I remember George Negus telling me when we were two up, 'You were right'.

"But, football being football, things happen and sometimes they go against you. All the time you see teams playing well and dominating the opposition and then one mistake at the other end and they are behind.

"Mackay had tears running down his face after the final whistle. We were all shattered.

"Many critics offered several explanations for the debilitating debacle, but for me Rasic hit the nail on the head when he said that he would not have allowed the team to be so tactically naive in the latter stages of the game."

Rasic of course would have been mystified by the Socceroos' refusal to sit back, protect their lead and see out the match.

"I think the Socceroos were so comfortable that night that they felt they were under no threat from the Iranians and opted not to change their cavalier approach," Alston said. "They were enjoying themselves too much.

"Had Rasic been in charge though, the Australians would have managed those last minutes much better. The ball would have been out of play very often, I can tell you."

Alston has nothing but praise for the stellar side coached by Dutchman Guus Hiddink that qualified for the 2006 finals and reached the round of 16 before they controversially fell to eventual winners Italy.

"I am reluctant to rank any of the Socceroos' sides that came after us because each had its strong points," he explained.

"All I will say is that the team comprising the 'golden generation' of 2006 was the best in that period.

"That side had some unbelievable players like Mark Viduka, Harry Kewell, Tim Cahill, Marco Bresciano and Lucas Neill who all played in Europe and it was such a relief to see the Socceroos team qualify for the first time in 32 years."

Alston also said he is an unabashed admirer of Ange Postecoglou, who famously led the Socceroos to their first major honour by landing the 2015 AFC Asian Cup on home soil.

"I thought Ange was awesome and did a fabulous job with the Socceroos, even though he did not have the luxury of many great players as other national coaches had."

"And what I liked about him is that he did things his own way and did not fall into the trap of changing for anybody else.

"For him to achieve that triumph with the Socceroos, then win the league championship in Japan and follow it up with more silverware in Scotland is amazing. He obviously has got some talent."

Alston also said he is suitably impressed with the work Graham Arnold did with the Socceroos in the 2022 World Cup in Qatar.

The Australians defied their critics and the form book by storming into the last 16 before giving former champions Argentina an almighty fright.

The Australians lost 2–1, but they had Lionel Messi and his amigos on the ropes in the last 15 minutes as they sought a goal that would have taken the match into extra time.

It was not to be, but the team's gallant performances throughout the tournament thrilled an entire nation and will not be forgotten easily by hundreds of thousands of Australians, especially those who attended several fan zones that were set up in all major cities.

"I thought we did extremely well in Qatar. Even qualifying for the finals at Peru's expense was a hell of an achievement and people should not lose sight of this," Alston said.

"It was disappointing to see the negative reaction to our first defeat against France. Many media personalities wrote off the team. It was the coach's fault because they were too defensive, they said. Blah, blah, blah.

"Give 'em a break, they were playing against France … the holders and favourites.

"To their credit, the Socceroos recovered in their next group matches against Tunisia and Denmark and gave us all a huge thrill by reaching the next phase. It was very emotional to see the boys deservedly win both games 1–0 and qualify for the next round against all the odds.

"Australia was in the last 16 of the World Cup for the second time in 16 years.

"It was not just 2006, though. Remember, we also reached the last 16 in 1974 when the competition had only 16 teams.

"It was just wonderful to watch the boys give everything in Qatar and I was glad to see their brave efforts rewarded. I was in tears after they beat the Danes because memories of my own participation in the World Cup came flooding back.

"It was just awesome to watch our boys give Argentina a hell of a run in the round of 16. At one goal down we were beginning to get back into the game and at that point anything could have happened, but the second goal killed us.

"We still had scoring chances, and I tell you, the Argentines were glad to hear the final whistle."

Alston has nothing but praise for the magnificent overall performance of striker Mathew Leckie, whose winning goal against Denmark provided one of the most memorable moments in Australia's football history.

"He was an impressive performer in every match and he showed his maturity as a footballer after spending a big part of his career in Germany," Alston said.

"He had many years playing against the best and he is now playing in Australia which is fantastic. Wouldn't it be wonderful if all the players who took part in the 2022 World Cup were able to play in the A-League?"

Alston said Arnold's ability to adapt to different opponents and various match situations was one of the reasons behind the team's stellar performance in Qatar. The Socceroos defended in numbers when they needed to but were never afraid to go on the front foot when the circumstances required a more adventurous approach. "It is a tactical balance that should provide the national team with more success," he said.

"We lost 4–1 to France but had we played an open game for 90 minutes, it could have been 10, so what would have been the point," Alston argued.

"Mind you, sometimes you have no say in the matter and you're powerless. The Aussies started strongly against the French but when Les Bleus took hold of the ball for the rest of the match and never stopped attacking, it was hard for our boys to get out of their area.

"What were our boys supposed to do, leave three at the back to face five attackers?

"Yet in the matches against Denmark and Argentina, the team was able to hold its nerve in sticky moments and have the strength of character to change the course of the match by going on the attack.

"This showed the team's ability to be tactically versatile, which was very satisfying to see. We don't have to be a defensive or attacking team … the best option is to be adaptable."

Alston said he has every reason to believe that the future of Australian football is looking promising, yet he stresses the importance of having a strong and viable club competition that is not seen as a poor relation to the AFL and NRL anymore.

"We need a strong and attractive league and I believe this can happen if we can make it appealing for more Aussie internationals to play here and perhaps sign a few strong foreigners, not some second division players.

"Our top competition needs to become more appealing to free-to-air television and cannot remain hidden away in streaming services that do not enjoy a big audience.

"We need to aim higher and seek a wider exposure for our game and not rest on our laurels after the Socceroos' success in Qatar. We cannot afford to make the same mistakes we have made in the past."

Alston believes the women's game is in the same boat.

The Matildas' exploits in the last few years, culminating in their impressive surge to the 2023 World Cup semi-finals, alerted him to the giant strides made by Australia's women footballers.

Alston admits he was not always a big fan of the women's game but like so many thousands he came around as overall standards improved.

He of course knows first-hand how hard it is to compete with the game's best teams on a world stage.

"The gap in quality between club football and the World Cup is enormous and I take my hat off to the Matildas for giving the tournament a real shake before going down to a very strong England side," he says.

"In my playing days for South Coast and St George I could see the huge disparity in playing standards between the local league and international football.

"So for the Matildas to perform so well on the world stage is truly remarkable.

"Their success—and the massive following they generated right across Australia— has set up the women's game for a bright and rewarding future because there will be so many young children wanting to play the game and try to be the next Sam Kerr or Mary Fowler.

"Kerr is a wonderful striker and the fantastic goal she scored against England confirmed her status as one of the world's finest players. I tell you, I would have been proud to score a goal like that.

"And what about young Fowler, my favourite player in the team? She is an exquisite player who will play a major part in our game for many years. She is very impressive."

Same as in the men's A-League, however, the women's competition has considerable obstacles to overcome on its journey towards sustainability and long-term credibility. Many gifted players, for example, are forced to play overseas because the local game cannot support them financially.

The respective domestic competitions are therefore shorn of the country's best talent.

"When you watch rugby league you can see the best players in the world week in week out. Yet they do not fill their grounds except for State of Origin," Alston argues.

"It is therefore difficult for our football clubs to draw big crowds because the fans want to see the best talent, after all.

"So how on earth can our clubs pay the kind of money some of our Socceroos and Matildas can earn abroad?"

Alston firmly believes that the Socceroos in Qatar in 2022 and the Matildas in Australia in 2023 have shown in no uncertain ways that they are strong enough to compete and with solid support from Football Australia they could become a "constant" force in the world game not a one-tournament wonder.

"Events of the last year have definitely given football in Australia a dramatic lift," he says.

"Our game has had many false dawns over the years but I have no doubt that this time we're in business.

"Johnny Warren was right, you know … football is finally becoming a major sport in Australia.

"He did tell us."

Chapter 24
The last word: Thanks for everything, Boss

Adrian Alston's colourful story would not be complete without a personal tribute to the late Rale Rasic, the man who helped him achieve the impossible dream of playing in the World Cup.

Alston and Rasic go a long way, having crossed paths for the first time in 1970.

Both had a deep and mutual respect and admiration for each other.

"Rale's passing did not come as a complete shock because we all knew he was ill but when it did come on the morning of 8 June it felt like a bit of me was lost forever," Alston says.

"I first met Rale when he became St George coach in 1970 at about the same time he was appointed as Socceroos boss. He was only 34 and looked very young. I found him to be quite straightforward; there was no bullshit about him which is something I appreciated very much. He always said it the same way he meant it.

"The Boss was the same man on and off the field. Simply because his life was football. Whenever we met socially, we talked about nothing else but football. It was discussion after discussion on the game we both loved so much.

"To be perfectly honest I was disappointed to see Arok quit St George in 1970 but when Rale came in, he soon showed his worth because he had no problem managing a Saints team that was full of international players. He quickly established himself as the boss.

"Character was very important to Rale. He always said, 'I don't pick the player, I pick the man'. He expected a player to play to the best of his ability but also to be loyal to his teammates and show full commitment to the cause. When I got to know him really well after many years and started asking him why he did this and that I found out things about him. You discovered what his values really were.

"I have several fond memories of Rale.

"Oddly enough my fondest was not the 1974 World Cup but the four-team tournament in Tokyo which we won two years earlier. That's when I think I really jelled with him. It was the moment I began to fully understand what he needed from me and that was when he gave me the freedom to do my thing up front because he started to fully appreciate my qualities. That tournament was when I became very close to Rale.

"Rale was like a father figure to us. He was always concerned about our needs outside of football. Even towards the end he was ringing 'his' players from 1974 and asking them if they were okay or if they needed anything.

"I was already an established player when Rale and I crossed paths in 1970. I was doing well enough to earn a transfer to St George but looking back at my career he used to annoy me sometimes whenever he took me off for no apparent reason … but in time I learned to appreciate his tactical genius.

"Did I get on with him all the time? The answer is 'no'. I had plenty of feelings about him because he was a bastard. I missed out on a starting role in several World Cup qualifiers and it was not the first time he took me off after scoring twice and I was chasing a hat-trick, for example. Many times I thought he was wrong but the whole point is to win a game and now that I'm much older I can understand why he did what he did.

"I wish I listened to him more.

"At the completion of our involvement in the 1974 World Cup, Hertha Berlin was showing serious interest in signing me but some officials from Eintracht Frankfurt caught up with me at a railway station and asked me to join them in a private room to talk about a contract offer. But my mind was already set on the highest level of English football. I was on my own with an interpreter and at one stage Rale knocked on the door and asked me if I needed any assistance. I said, 'I'm fine, Rale'. Which was probably a mistake. I should have let him in because he could have persuaded me to go to Germany instead of England. Rale would remind me many times over the years that I had made a big mistake. And he was right.

"He was very often a pain in the arse but, my word, he was such a talented man, very intelligent and university educated. He came through a tough upbringing in the former Yugoslavia which probably best explains why he was so considerate and why he achieved so much as a man manager.

"I went to see him in hospital a few days before he died. He was very ill but he talked a lot and would not let go of my hand. In the half an hour or so that I was with him he kept asking about the players of 1974 that meant so much to him. He wanted to know about all of them, one by one. 'How is Willie going?' 'What about Bunny?' 'And Dougie?' he asked.

"It was heartbreaking and I left with tears in my eyes.

"The Boss was a very special man."

Acknowledgements

The compilation of such a long and fascinating story as that of high-profile Socceroos star Adrian Alston would not have been possible without the striker's unflinching willingness to spend many hours talking about his extraordinary life.

'Noddy' is a natural story teller yet often he had to fall back on his memory when it came to some of the lesser-known moments that defined his career, and when his memory failed him there was always the 'get-out-of-jail' card called Rale Rasic. The late mentor was always able to clarify and confirm any issues that might have been clouded by time. He also was only too happy to provide the Foreword for this book.

Last but not least, sincere thanks should go to Fair Play Publishing for believing in this project from day one. I hope that this book will form an important part in the colourful quilt that is Australian football history and culture.

About the Author

Philip Micallef is a retired sports journalist who has worked for Fairfax, News Ltd, and SBS (The World Game).

He has covered many major football events such as the World Cup, the European Championships, the Copa America, the UEFA and AFC Champions League tournaments plus dozens of Socceroos, the National League, and A-League matches. He also has interviewed enough top footballers to be able to compile a strong 'World XI'.

He is also the author of *'The World Cup Story, An Australian View'* (1994) and *'Quote, Unquote'* (Fair Play Publishing, 2022).

Philip, who was born in Malta, migrated to Australia in 1981 and lives in Sydney with his wife Maria. They have two adult children.

MORE REALLY GOOD FOOTBALL BOOKS FROM FAIR PLAY PUBLISHING

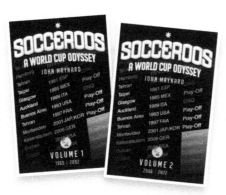

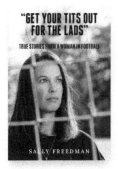
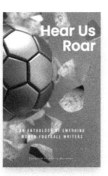
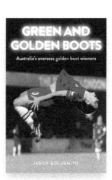

FAIRPLAY

PUBLISHING

www.fairplaypublishing.com.au

Milton Keynes UK
Ingram Content Group UK Ltd.
UKHW020654151123
432603UK00003B/10